How to Grow Your Own
Fruit and Veg

How to Grow Your Own
Fruit and Veg

A week-by-week guide to wild-life friendly fruit and vegetable gardening

SECOND EDITION

Joe Hashman

SPRING HILL

Published by Spring Hill

Spring Hill is an imprint of
How To Books Ltd
Spring Hill House
Spring Hill Road
Begbroke
Oxford
OX5 1RX
Tel: (01865) 375794
Fax: (01865) 379162

info@howtobooks.co.uk
www.howtobooks.co.uk

First published 2007 (as How To Grow Your Own Food)
Reprinted 2007
Reprinted 2008 (twice)
Reprinted 2009
Second edition 2012

British Library Cataloguing in Publication Data
A catalogue record of this book is available from the British Library

ISBN: 978-1-905862-77-1

Cover Design by Mousemat Design Ltd

Produced for How To Books by
Deer Park Productions, Tavistock
Designed and typeset by Mousemat Design Ltd
Printed and bound by Bell & Bain Ltd, Glasgow

NOTE: The material contained in this book is set out in good faith
for general guidance and no liability can be accepted for loss or
expense incurred as a result of relying in particular circumstances on
statements made in the book. Laws and regulations are complex and
liable to change, and readers should check the current position with
relevant authorities before making personal arrangements.

ld like to acknowledge the
ring people who have been
mental in helping to make
eam of producing this
a reality:

Lewis, Nikki Read and all
w To Books, for their
ous help and support in
this venture.

My wife, for her unconditional
love and brilliant company.

CONTENTS

CONTENTS

INTRODUCTION

Everyone, regardless of background, status or class ultimately depends on the land for survival.

It is this basic instinctive need that first inspired me to start growing food. My efforts have nothing to do with cultivating the largest, roundest, shiniest onion or longest, straightest runner bean. Such pastimes are for others. The passion I feel is simply for eating good honest food whilst simultaneously following the natural order of things on the plot, tuning in to the ebb and flow of life beyond computer screens and outside of walls and windows.

To feel the sun across my back or rain in my face, to cut a lettuce in midsummer or gather lovingly tended produce for a deep-winter feast in icy conditions with freezing hands and fingers red raw – this is the stuff of my dreams.

I want to be at one with the elements, to feel my place in the never ending cycle of life death and rebirth, to commune with the amazing diversity of plants and creatures that come and go with the changing seasons. If you allow them, it is these magical ingredients which combine to make the edible gardening experience such an exquisite one.

No two years are the same in the fruit and veg patch. The weather, pests and diseases and our own personal circumstances are unpredictable and ever changing. But this book is a guide to what you might achieve in the next twelve months. It's also a source of tips and information to be revisited again and again.

Whoever you are and wherever you live, *How to Grow Your Own Fruit and Veg* is designed to help you achieve just that and have the time of your life whilst doing it!

LEEKS

Varieties

Now is the time to start thinking about your leeks. I like to get mine on the go as early as possible. To this end, sowing seeds of an autumn variety in trays this week is a good idea. Carentan 2 is ideal. Musselburg is another popular one to try.

Sowing seeds

Sow the small black seeds thinly in a tray of potting compost and cover lightly. These will do well if kept moist, and set on a window-sill indoors until the grass-like shoots appear.

It won't take too many days.

Managing seedlings

It is always a thrill when the first leeks start sprouting. Trays of bristling seedlings can go into the greenhouse at this stage, and then be planted out into a nursery bed from about the end of March (see April, 2nd Week).

I always over-do it with my leeks. But this is good, because half the crop can be dug up and eaten for a sweet tasting baby leek treat around the middle of July.

NATURAL HISTORY IN THE GARDEN
Badgers in February

Badgers that live close by will be giving birth at this time of year. Two or three cubs is the usual number per female, and they spend the first eight weeks or so in their underground breeding chamber. This will be lined with soft dried vegetation which the badgers collect from around and about. When they are cleaning out these chambers, or bringing in fresh bedding, debris is often left scattered in the vicinity of their hole, or 'sett'. Such evidence of badgers is particularly noticeable this month.

VEGETABLE SNIPPETS
A BRIEF HISTORY OF
THE LEEK

The leek, *Allium porrum*, occurs naturally across a region that stretches all the way from Israel to India, and has been cultivated as an important food source since at least 3500 BC. Its distribution throughout Europe was assured by the Ancient Egyptians, Greeks and Romans. The latter, who brought leeks to Britain after AD 43, knew leeks as *porrum*. After their Empire collapsed in AD 410 this crop, along with cabbages (brassicas) and beans (pulses), became an important dietary ingredient throughout the British and European Dark Ages. In Saxon times leeks were widely grown. The Anglo-Saxon term 'laec tun', which actually means 'leek enclosure', can be found today in both family and place names, including Layton, Leighton, Latham, Lighton and Letton.

Leeks were exported to the so-called New World. By 1775 both settlers and Native Americans were raising leeks for the pot in what was to become the United States. Back in the UK this member of the onion tribe remained popular through the Little Ice Age that took place between the sixteenth and nineteenth centuries, when it was happily able to withstand the drop in temperatures as a 'standing crop' (left in the fields and dug as required in winter).

Often overlooked in more recent times, leeks offer a gourmet meal when cooked gently until tender. The French, notorious as connoisseurs of fine foods, are apt to compare a well prepared dish of leeks with that much sought-after delicacy, asparagus.

PATHS

When wet weather puts the kibosh on digging and ground preparation why not turn your attention to paths in the vegetable garden instead? Wooden planks are all very well for temporary access to crops, but where regular routes are walked something more solid will make life easier in the months to come.

Easy construction with bricks

I like to construct rustic paths with old bricks and gather them wherever I can, including skips and dumps. Only unbroken ones will do. Lay them side-by-side across, and set them out as the path will go. Then simply use a spade to dig out two-thirds the depth of the brick, and break up the bottom of the trench. Move the bricks to one side as you do this, and place them back in as you progress with about 1.25 cm or so between them. They will settle comfortably in the trench with the stamp of a foot. Your spade can be employed to scatter some of the excavated soil onto the bricks and a piece of wood used to scrape this into the cracks. Then ram it down with a thin edge. Finally, sweep clean.

The structure these paths give to the garden is very pleasing. They instantly blend in with a look of natural permanence. Walk and wheel-barrow as much as you like, as this all helps the bricks to nestle in. A path constructed thus can be left for years, or shifted with a minimum of fuss and disruption as the garden evolves.

NATURAL HISTORY IN THE GARDEN
Wild Arum

Lush, deep green whorls of leaves are popping up in the unkempt garden edges. They belong to the wild arum, which is also known as 'cuckoo pint', or 'lords and ladies'. This is a fascinating wild flower with a very unusual way of reproducing. From the centre it sends up a smelly brown spike which attracts insects. These are captured by the plant and held hostage overnight by one-way, hair-like triggers. When pollination via the insects has occurred the triggers wither, and the captives are released unharmed. All this excitement happens in April and May. For now, the fresh bundles of growth are just a promise of the natural magic to come.

VEGETABLE SNIPPETS

LIVING WITH
TRAVELLING BADGERS

Paths should be constructed so as to allow comfortable wheelbarrow access. Making them too narrow will result in awkward manoeuvring of this essential piece of kit. When crops are in the ground, especially once well into the growing season, they can flop over a narrow path. This not only causes damp trouser bottoms in wet weather, but also potentially damages the crop itself through bruising as the gardener brushes past. A nice, wide path is a pleasure, one that is tight a pain.

Creating regularly used and well-worn routes is not a condition restricted just to humans. Badgers and deer are also creatures of habit. If they are resident in the area of the veg plot, evidence of their night-time wanderings will be conspicuous. Badgers are apt to use the same paths from their home to foraging sites over generations. A patch or scrape of bare soil under a fence is tell-tale. The discovery of coarse white-tipped black and white hairs caught on thorns or barbed wire hereabouts is even stronger evidence of them passing to and fro. It is very difficult to dissuade badgers from using their favourite paths. Blocking their way can prove both frustrating (to the gardener) and damaging (to the fence).

In this situation I'd advise installing a sturdy two-way gate. It works along the lines of a small-dog sized cat flap. Alternatively, a gap can be left which will allow these handsome nocturnal beasts free passage as they like.

BEAN TRENCHES AND LETTUCE

February, 3rd Week

A good site for beans

I've just finished filling the second of my runner bean trenches with compostable kitchen waste. Trodden down, then covered with the excavated soil, the decomposing organic matter will ensure plenty of goodness for this summer's runners. My trenches have been dug along a shed and fence that receives plenty of sun, because I like to grow runner beans as an edible screen.

Trench composting

'Trench composting' consists of digging a ditch one spit deep (depth of a spade head) and filling it with rottable refuse. Discarded vegetable matter can be added bit by bit over time and will break down slowly. When the trench is full, cover over with soil. Locked-up goodness is gradually released below the soil surface in the 'root zone'. This is exactly where crops, including hungry beans, want nourishment most. Runner bean seedlings will eventually be planted outside in mid-May at 20 cm intervals, so the trench must be dug to the desired length according to the number of individuals that are to be grown.

Well-rotted farmyard manure (FYM) can be used also for this method of feeding veggies. It is a superb alternative to the contents of the compost bucket, but can be a little harder to come by these days.

Sowing lettuces

In the greenhouse, or indoors, now's the time to sow lettuces. Talia (an Iceberg variety) Salad Bowl

NATURAL HISTORY IN THE GARDEN
Woodpeckers

Woodpeckers are making a noise this month. They will be busy in surrounding big trees, communicating with each other. Both the greater and lesser spotted varieties use trees as sounding boards. The greater has distinctive red feathers at the base of its tail. It is both bigger and more common than the blackbird-sized lesser. The drumming noise is made by rapid blows of their beaks on branches, and up to ten drums can occur per second. Greater spotted 'peckers have a deep repeat which fades at the end. The lesser is higher pitched and stops abruptly.

VEGETABLE SNIPPETS

A LOOK AT
THE LETTUCE

(cut-and-come-again) or Lobjoits Green Cos are ideal for sowing now in trays of moist compost. As soon as the second pair of true leaves have formed get them out into the sunniest spot possible. Pegging plastic bells over these first outdoor lettuces will bring them on a treat. With a bit of luck these lettuces could be ready for picking or cutting and eating by late April or early May. That'll be one of those early-season moments that makes life worth living.

Lactuca serriola still grows all over Europe, North Africa and the temperate parts of Asia. This plant is the wild predecessor of all the multitude of different types of cultivated lettuce. In Britain it is commonly known as 'prickly lettuce'. The Ancient Egyptians are believed to have been the first to begin domesticating this plant. Lettuce was extremely popular by Roman times. Known back then as 'vinegar salads', they were served as a first course at banquets, and eaten with great gusto on account of the supposed aphrodisiac qualities

contained within their leaves. By the fourteenth century lettuces were being widely cultivated in Britain.

As well as being nutritionally useful sources of vitamins A, C and B9 (folic acid), potassium and iron, lettuces also contain small amounts of a narcotic not dissimilar to opium. It is this which has earned these leafy saladings their reputation for aiding restful sleep. In Beatrix Potter's story *The Tale of the Flopsy Bunnies* the rabbits who raided Mr McGregor's vegetable patch succumbed to these soporific qualities.

JERUSALEM ARTICHOKES

February, 4th Week

A sensible site for Jerusalem artichokes
Personally, I like to get my Jerusalem artichokes into the ground as soon as soils are workable in the New Year, but any time until mid-March will suffice. Planting them at the back of the veg patch is a sensible idea, in a line that won't cast shade on other crops. Jerusalem artichokes are very dense of growth, and thus ideal for screening off unsightly compost heaps or fences.

Preparing and planting
Incorporate leafmould and grass clippings by digging them into the soil. Then plant your artichokes, saved from a previous crop or simply brought from the grocers, 30 cm apart and 12.5 cm deep. This valuable vegetable will grow in the poorest conditions, but a little tender loving care will repay with a fine crop of knobbly tubers (the edible underground stem).

Subsequent husbandry
All the plants need is to be kept watered and weed-free. Earth-up around the base when there is about 30 cm of growth. Cut off a third of the tops after mid-summer, to prevent wind-rock. At the end of August I always reduce the top growth by half.

Harvesting and storing
Harvesting can commence any time from November. One plant is dug at a time, and the bounty stored in boxes of damp sand until needed. Ten plants should keep a family of four comfortably supplied all winter.

NATURAL HISTORY IN THE GARDEN
Song Thrush

Listen out for the song thrush enriching an otherwise dull February landscape. They like to perch high up in big lime trees. Their early morning song is a repetitive series of beautiful, tuneful, fluting, liquid notes and elaborate musical clicks and whistles, punctuated by short, well-timed pauses. The speckle-breasted birds open their beaks widely and constantly turn their heads whilst delivering this chorus, providing a musical treat for the listener.

VEGETABLE SNIPPETS
JERUSALEM ARTICHOKES DEMYSTIFIED

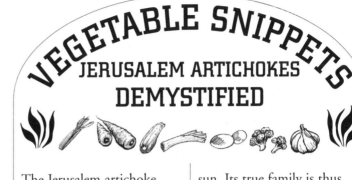

The Jerusalem artichoke (*Helianthus tuberosus*) is neither from Jerusalem, nor an artichoke. In fact this vegetable heralds from North America. It was a staple foodstuff for Native Americans from Nova Scotia in the east to Minnesota and Kansas, well before Columbus 'discovered' the continent.

'Jerusalem' is believed to be a corruption of *girasola*, which in Italian means 'turning towards the sun'. This refers to the habit of the pretty yellow flowers, about 6 cm in diameter, which like to open into the sun. Its true family is thus revealed: the Jerusalem artichoke is in fact a relative of the sunflower.

Nutritionally high in iron, potassium, and thiamine, and alternatively known as the 'sunchoke', or 'sun root', the Jerusalem was being marketed in Europe by the early 1600s. At that time it was called the Canada, or French, potato. It was also introduced to Britain around then, along with such delicacies as cultivated straw-berries, different beans, gourds, sweet peppers and tomatoes.

BROAD BEANS

March, 1st Week

This week you could be planting broad beans. The productive and very early Witkeim variety is my choice for sowing at this time of year.

Planting depth and distances

The seeds are large, browny-grey and feel substantial in your hand. Children of all ages love planting them. Place the magical pieces on the surface of evenly raked, weed-free soil in a line at 12 cm intervals. If you fancy sowing a double row then allow 20 cm between lines.

When you've set your seeds out as desired, gently press them into the soil end-on to a depth of 5 cm and cover them over. If it is cold then I might be minded to place cloches over the top to keep the seedbed warmer.

Home-grown broads really do taste completely different to shop-bought, and are highly nutritious. With luck, a sowing this week will be producing pods of fat beans around mid-summer.

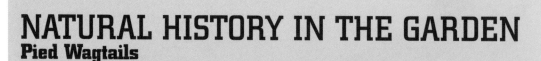

NATURAL HISTORY IN THE GARDEN
Pied Wagtails

Small black and white birds with long black flicking-up tails and a low, undulating, dancy flight, are pied wagtails. They gather on the lawn in ones and twos, sometimes more. The pied wagtail bobs its head back and fore as it quarters the ground with rapid darting runs, occasionally jumping up acrobatically to snaffle low-flying insects.

VEGETABLE SNIPPETS

SOME FACTS ABOUT
THE BROAD BEAN

Scientifically, the broad bean is *Vicia faba*, also known as the 'fava bean'. Horse bean or field bean are other alternatives, although these last two names generally refer to crops that are commonly grown as animal fodder. Broads popular for human consumption nowadays are larger-seeded varieties. Native to North Africa and Southwest Asia, these beans are believed to have comprised part of the European diet even before 6000 BC. They were particularly popular in the Stone Age Mediterranean region. European folklore has it that planting this crop either on Good Friday or at night-time is a harbinger of good luck.

Broad beans are rich in protein, so much so that they have been called 'vegetable meat'. Vitamins A and C are readily available, so too phosphorous. Broads contain the cancer fighting substance lectin, so may help in this department also.

PARSNIPS

March, 2nd Week

When to sow

Parsnips can be sown any time from mid-February until early May, just so long as the soil feels comfortably warm. 'Snips prefer a deeply dug bed raked into a fine tilth, with as few stones as possible. White King is a variety which can produce large tender roots in these conditions. If your soil is rather shallow and/or stony, try Avonresister.

Preparation and planting

Having prepared the ground, mark out your rows, each one 30 cm apart. I like to station-sow my parsnip seeds at 15 cm intervals. This is a simple task which involves pushing a finger into the soil to a depth of 2 cm. Then three seeds are placed into each shallow hole, covered over and firmed gently. You'd be wise to choose a dry calm day for this, as even a slight breeze can cause the confetti-like seeds to become very hard to handle. When I'll be sowing a batch of Avonresister next month, I'll halve the planting distance because the roots are smaller.

Be patient!

Like most veg, 'snips like to be kept moist and weed-free. They are notoriously slow germinators. It may be over a month before the seedlings emerge from the

NATURAL HISTORY IN THE GARDEN
Daisies and Dandelions

The old saying goes that spring is truly sprung when a maiden can put her foot on seven daisies. That is sure to be the case in the days ahead on the lawn as these lovely little flowers start to really get going, popping up their cheery heads all over the place. The name daisy comes from 'day's eye', which sums up this low growing plant perfectly. In the bright sunshine they spread their petals to catch the rays, but close them up when it's dull and overcast.

Dandelions have been showing themselves shyly for a few weeks now, but they will be producing their sun-like yellow flower heads in profusion soon. These beautiful, bold flowers would surely be cherished more if they were not so common. They are especially valuable to bees and hoverflies that are on the wing in early spring.

soil. Be patient! Thin to the strongest seedling then and enjoy the wait. Roasted parsnip is a highlight of the long winter months.

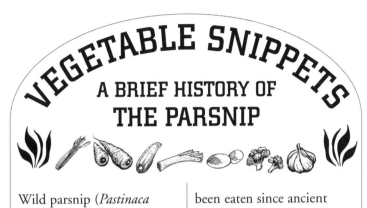

VEGETABLE SNIPPETS
A BRIEF HISTORY OF
THE PARSNIP

Wild parsnip (*Pastinaca saliva*) grows all over Britain on well drained grasslands and waste ground. It is most at home on alkaline chalky and limestone soils. Above ground, the flowers and foliage of the wild version are very similar to its well-bred, domesticated cousin. Indeed, biologically they are the same plant. However, selective breeding down the generations has differentiated them, and developed the fat root in one which is so popular in the kitchen.

Parsnips are native throughout Eurasia and have been eaten since ancient times. In fact until the sixteenth century, when potatoes arrived in Britain from the Americas, they were a staple part of the winter diet. Parsnips are rich in dietary fibre as well as numerous vitamins and minerals, especially potassium and calcium. It is exposure to cold temperatures which prompts starch in the root to become sugar. This desirable sweetness is the main reason why the advice traditionally is not to lift 'snips until after the first frost.

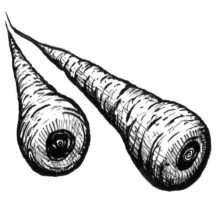

ONIONS

March, 3rd Week

Planting onion sets is a vegetable gardening highlight for early spring, especially if there is some warm morning sunshine across your back at the same time. It's a job I'll be aiming to complete this week.

Ground work
The onion bed should be thoroughly prepared beforehand, with leafmould and well rotted manure dug in, then wood ash raked in. I like to give my onion bed two or three good rakings before treading it all down lightly. Onions like a firm footing. Stuttgarter Giant, Sturon and Red Baron are all widely available as sets.

NATURAL HISTORY IN THE GARDEN
Badgers in March

The mating season for badgers gets into full swing during March, April and May, and continues until the autumn. However the females (sows) can hold fertilised eggs in their bodies in a kind of suspended animation, known as 'delayed implantation', until December. The embryonic badgers are then allowed to develop and are born around mid-January to mid-March. They enter the world virtually bald and will remain blind for the first five weeks of their lives.

VEGETABLE SNIPPETS

SOME FACTS ABOUT ONIONS

Planting depth and distances

Mark out your rows 30 cm apart and place the acorn-sized onions along these rows at 15 cm intervals. When they are in place it's simply a case of pushing each tiny onion into the soil leaving just the husky tip standing proud. Use your finger to make a little nest for each one, then firm it in. Keep an eye on them closely for the first week or so and press back any that are lifted by frost, birds, or their own sprouting roots. Keep moist and weed-free, watch the green shoots grow and the bulbs swell. It'll be well into August before you'll need to think about harvesting.

The Ancient Egyptians held that onions symbolised eternal life, supposedly on account of this bulbous vegetable's globular shape and the concentric rings concealed within its papery skin. Cultivation is believed to have commenced in that part of the world around 3000 BC and onions are one of the first domesticated crops ever to be written about.

Cultivated onions (*Allium cepa*) are just one of about 450 species in the allium family known about worldwide. Many, though by no means all, are edible. These days raising a harvest from sets, as opposed to seed, is considered to be a consistently reliable method of producing food in the kitchen garden or on the allotment. Sets are simply small onions, part-grown and then heat treated. Fewer varieties are available commercially compared to seeds and this does limit choice for the gardener. They are also a more expensive way of growing this veg although, in truth, only by a matter of pennies. However, the flip-side of this is that mass produced sets have democra-tised onion growing, enabling everyone the opportunity to be successful in nurturing a good crop of this most useful of veg.

RADISHES

Sowing

If it's warm, radish seeds can be sown directly into weed-free soil this week. Quick growing French Breakfast is a favourite. Sowing a batch every ten days or so in short lines will ensure a summer-long supply of chunky, peppery roots. Drills only need to be 2.5 cm deep. They can be grooved out of a level, raked bed using a trowel edge or with fingers.

Radish seeds are large enough to handle individually. Carefully place them in the bottom of your drill at 5 cm intervals. Brush soil over the top of them with the back of your hand. Then gently firm, or 'tamp', the covered drill with the back of a rake. Apply water with the rose on your can. Radishes are thirsty veg and like to be grown in soil kept moist. The French Breakfast variety is prolific and incredibly good for you. Sown individually, thinning is kept to a minimum, and therefore so too is wastage.

When to pull

I'd advise you to pull your radishes when they are showing their bright red shoulders proud out of the soil and are approximately 5 cm in cylindrical length, which should be in a few short weeks time.

NATURAL HISTORY IN THE GARDEN
Jackdaws

Look out for members of the crow family congregating in numbers this month. A dozen or more jackdaws may hang out in tall trees overlooking the garden, watching keenly for a feeding opportunity. These handsome black and grey fellows are highly intelligent, sociable creatures. When one jack' sees the coast clear to land and have a poke about, it will soon be joined by others. They eat whatever they can find in the way of kitchen scraps, seeds, fruit, insects, carrion, plus other birds' eggs and nestlings in season.

VEGETABLE SNIPPETS

A RUNDOWN ON RADISHES

Radishes (*Raphanus sativus*) are related to cabbages. Therefore, although a quick and easy crop to grow, they should be spared from sowing on ground either side of cultivating kale, purple sprouting broccoli, Brussels sprouts and the like. This is in order to allow the soil time to recover fertility, and break the life cycle of any of the many pests and diseases which are prone to afflict this family of foodstuffs. Having said that, radishes kept uniformly moist (but not wet) are otherwise generally very rewarding. Predation by slugs, snails and flea beetles are the only major problems that I've encountered with them.

The first domesticated radishes are believed to have originated in China many moons ago. French Breakfast is an old heirloom variety which has been widely grown since the late 1800's on account of the beautiful looking, peppery tasting, red and white roots. Nutritionally high in potassium and vitamin C, radishes are wont to 'bolt' (flower and set seed) in dry conditions. If this happens the young seed pods can be pinched off and eaten as a tasty nibble.

GLOBE ARTICHOKES

March, 5th Week

Where to grow them
Globe Artichokes are considered a luxury in some circles, but their exquisite taste and fascinating growth make them an essential part of my veg plot. This edible thistle is generally easy to grow and, if space is tight, they'll be quite happy at the back of a flower border too.

Starting from seed
Why not get in to the greenhouse this week and sow seeds of the Green Globe variety. Bluish-grey and the size of a sunflower seed, they are simply nestled 1.5 cm deep into potting compost. Around mid-summer the young plants should be ready for planting out. In subsequent years, when big bud production is in full swing, globe artichokes will make a bushy clump of coarse, silvery-green leaves which like space, moisture and sunshine, so give them plenty of room to grow. One metre may seem excessive when small plants are less than a year old but your rewards will come.

How to cut and cook
Control yourself in the year after sowing. Harvest only the main, or 'king', bud. Pinch the smaller buds out before they come to anything. In subsequent years each plant should produce over half a dozen buds the size of a fist. These are cut, with a portion of stem attached, from June to October before the globes begin to open. Boiled until tender, there is a mouthful of artichoke flesh to be scraped from the bottom of each bud 'leaf', and a gorgeous 'heart' within to be savoured. The hairy 'choke', however, must be avoided.

Raising future plants
To ensure a succession of plants that are at their peak

NATURAL HISTORY IN THE GARDEN
Brimstone Butterfly

A warm spell this month will tempt the first butterflies out of hibernation. Keep an eye out for the brimstone, which over-winters in its adult form under loose bark, in thick ivy, or other frost-free hidey-holes. Its lovely plain yellow colouration, slightly paler on females, is what puts the 'butter' into butterfly.

I'd suggest raising a few seeds each year. Alternatively, knifing-away side growths with some root attached from strong plants in their three or four year-old prime. These suckers, taken in autumn or spring, are replanted and treated as one year-olds.

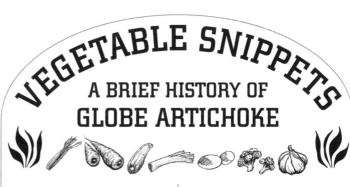

VEGETABLE SNIPPETS
A BRIEF HISTORY OF
GLOBE ARTICHOKE

It is thought that globe artichokes originated in the Mediterranean. There is evidence that this plant was being cultivated for food in Italy and Sicily from about 300 BC. The Greeks and Romans are credited with exporting globes further afield. The fact that *Cynara scolymus*, as it is known scientifically, does best when afforded a sizeable plot to grow in and produces a relatively small return for this space meant that at this time it was homed mainly in the aristocratic gardens of Europe. Here, globe artichokes achieved gourmet status and were highly prized on account of their reputed aphrodisiac and breath-freshening qualities. Globes were introduced to Britain in the sixteenth century.

Considered by many to be a luxury vegetable, these artichokes are nutritionally rich in vitamin C, folic acid, potassium and dietary fibre. Green Globe is one of the most popular of many varieties available today and hails from America.

SCORZONERA, SALSIFY AND POT MARIGOLDS

Early April is the time to get stuck in to digging, raking and sowing on the veg plot.

Sowing scorzonera
Scorzonera is an ancient vegetable, a particular favourite of mine which can be planted at any time from now until mid-May. The black, thong-like root may penetrate so deep that digging it out in one piece becomes a personal challenge. It is delicious eaten raw, steamed or baked.

Because of the length of root it makes sense to sow scorzonera in a deeply dug bed which is as stone-free as possible. The seeds resemble large grains of rice and are sown at 15 cm intervals, 4 cm deep. Sow two seeds at a time and thin to the strongest seedling as soon as the grass-like shoots have arched out of the soil. Scorzonera is simple to grow. All it demands is to be kept moist and weed free. Roots will stand

happily in the ground all winter for digging out as and when required.

Sowing salsify
Salsify is a root veg that resembles a large white carrot and has a delectable flavour. Cultivate it in exactly the same way as for scorzonera. Two or three 3 metre lines of both salsify and scorzonera should be ample for even the hungriest family of four.

NATURAL HISTORY IN THE GARDEN
Ornamental Purple Plum and Small Tortoiseshell Butterfly

Ornamental purple plum
Ornamental purple plum trees are at their peak early in the month. Delicate pale pink blossom feathers the branches like a dusting of rose-tinted snow. They soon give way to dark maroon leaves and the show is quickly over.

The small tortoiseshell butterfly
All manner of insects will be on the wing. A commonly observed butterfly is the small tortoiseshell. It has orange and dark brown wings, bordered on the back-facing edge with eye-catching half-moons. They will be laying eggs on the underside of nettle leaves as May approaches, which will hopefully lead to a new small tortoiseshell generation around midsummer. Fine weather is often the order of the day if butterflies are visible doing their rounds before nine o'clock in the morning.

April, 1st Week

Planting pot marigolds

Sow pot marigolds around the outside of your veg plot. The petals are edible and provide a beautiful garnish to salads or hot dishes.

Scatter the seeds as required and cover with a fine layer of soil. Thin them out in stages so that the young leaves are not touching. The resulting riot of orange and yellow flowers, which bloom continually throughout summer and autumn, create a glorious bee and insect-rich arena for the vegetables growing within.

VEGETABLE SNIPPETS

SALSIFY IN THE WILD AND SOME SCORZONERA FACTS

Salsify

Salsify grows wild in Britain as *Trapogon pratensis*, commonly known as Jack-go-to-bed-at-noon. This descriptive name refers to the yellow daisy-like flower. It is borne on a slender, grass-like stalk, opens early in the morning throughout high-summer and closes by noon. It sets seed by forming a 'clock' similar to a dandelion, only bigger and with chunkier seeds. They are spread via the wind, carried away with the aid of a parachute comprising a disc of feathery hairs.

In olden days the root of this plant was boiled in milk and given as a tonic to folk who were recovering from illness. Cultivated salsify differs only in that the delicate bloom is purple.

Scorzonera

Scorzonera (*Scorzonera hispanica*) heralds from Southern Europe and the Near East. Its widespread status can be attributed to the Spanish who exported this impressive root vegetable far and wide. The name 'scorzonera' comes from Old French, which was the spoken language a thousand years ago of Northern France, Belgium and Switzerland. It means 'snake'. The long, black tap root is indeed serpent-like, and traditionally this plant was used to treat snake bites. Other names include 'black oyster plant', 'Spanish salsify', 'serpent root', 'viper's grass'.

Scorzonera is a favourite food-plant of a common resident moth known as The Nutmeg (*Discestra trifolii*). The adults of this insect are superficially just earthy-brown in colour, but close inspection reveals a wonderful array of patterns and marbling. Night-flying adults are attracted to nectar-rich flowers, sugar and light. As juveniles the larvae are called cutworms. Later broods will over-winter in the topsoil within delicate, bullet-shaped cocoons. These may be turned up whilst harvesting scorzonera roots throughout winter.

LEEKS AND LETTUCES

April, 2nd Week

Planting leeks into a nursery

This week the time should be right for planting baby autumn leeks outside into a nursery bed. For this, rake the soil in your bed to a fine tilth, and then moisten it. Use a rose-ended watering can or sprinkler hose if the soil is dry. Then mark out the rows with canes and string to your desired length. If planting up more than one row, make them 15 cm apart. Make holes along each row with a pencil, bamboo cane or straight twig, at 8 cm intervals and 5 cm deep.

The leeks, which each look like a thin strand of grass, will have two or three long trailing roots. They need to be eased gently out of their seed tray and carefully teased apart. Extra-long roots can be trimmed by a half with no ill effects. Then drop in one leek per hole. Make sure the roots are as nestled down as possible and not poking out of the top. You might find that turning the baby leek between your fingers as you plant it helps to prevent this. They are then 'puddled in', which means that they are watered directly in their holes. Again, use a watering can fitted with a rose. Soil falls naturally over the roots and should be nicely bedded in after a few such puddlings. When your leeks have grown to pencil thickness after mid-summer, they will be ready to go into the leek bed proper, or eaten as they are, young and sweet.

NATURAL HISTORY IN THE GARDEN
Badgers in April

Badgers are very active this month. Young cubs born in February, now fully furred and with eyes wide open, will be tempted to have a peek out from the mouth of their sett entrance and sniff the air above ground. If family groups are crowded, fighting can occur at this time of year. Last season's boars (males), who are low down in the pecking order, may be driven out. It is a noisy affair, with vicious squabbling sometimes leading to nasty injuries, especially under the rump. Displaced badgers will have to make their own way in the world from now on. These brutal encounters can sound prehistoric as they scrap, roll and tumble in the darkness amongst the brambles and undergrowth.

VEGETABLE SNIPPETS

LETTUCE CHAT

Planting out lettuces

Greenhouse-grown lettuces such as Lobjoits Green Cos, Talia and Buttercrunch are ready to be planted outside now. Placing plastic bells over these transplanted lettuces keeps them growing fast when the weather can still be a bit nippy. Lettuces need about 20 cm between plants, and like to be kept sunny and moist. Salad days will soon be here, especially if the odd juicy leaf is taken early.

Lettuces are the food plant for numerous species of moth whose grub-like larvae are collectively known as 'cutworms'. Though some are considered to be damaging, viewing cutworms as a valuable part of the garden ecology is more helpful. Adult moths are lovely. Those for whom lettuces are enjoyed in early life include the Large Yellow Underwing, Garden Dart, Common Swift and the Angle Shades. The latter is common throughout Britain and, despite the fact that it over-winters as a cocoon just below the soil surface, adults may be seen on the wing during any month of the year.

Cos lettuces form crisp heads of elongated leaves. They are alternatively known as Romaine lettuces.

Iceberg lettuces are also called Crisphead lettuces. Their dense, round heads do not look unlike a cabbage. Home-grown icebergs are a pleasure and treat to eat with their wonderful crunchy texture and distinctive, cooling flavour.

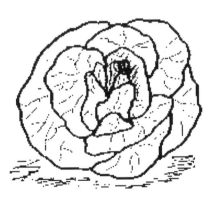

BEETROOT AND COURGETTES

April, 3rd Week

This is the perfect time to start sowing beetroot, so why not get some seeds on the go this week? Detroit 2 is a good variety to try, or Boltardy. Putting down a 2 metre line every fortnight from now until July will hopefully ensure a steady supply of golfball-sized, sweet-yet-earthy roots from mid-summer and through the autumn. In June and July also sow the long-rooted Cylindra. This variety has an extra intense flavour and a beautiful texture when boiled until tender.

Sowing beetroot seeds

Beetroot seeds are small and knobbly. They should be sown thinly not more than 2.5 cm deep. Allow 30 cm between each line. Germination can be anything from a few days to a fortnight or so, depending on the weather. Detroit 2 and Cylindra seeds are multi-germ, which means that each one may produce two, three or four seedlings. These should be thinned to the strongest as soon as they are big enough to handle.

Thin again when leaves are touching. Aim for 13 cm betwixt individuals for big beets, or less for smaller portions.

Starting courgettes in the greenhouse

Start your courgettes off now, either in the greenhouse or on a window-sill. Pop the large, flat, oval seeds on edge, 2.5 cm deep into 7.5 cm pots full of potting compost. Kept moist, they should grow on nicely, and will be gradually hardened off

NATURAL HISTORY IN THE GARDEN
Cuckoo arrival

April is the month for keeping an early morning or evening ear out for the cuckoo. These birds return to Britain from Africa in the late spring to breed, and will hopefully be arriving around the 15th. Males sing the unmistakable 'cu-coo' which is so evocative of England as summer beckons. The female has a completely different call, a water-bubbling chuckle. For now, cuckoos will be focusing on recovering from their long overseas migration, feeding up and finding a mate.

VEGETABLE SNIPPETS

A BRIEF HISTORY OF
THE BEETROOT

prior to planting out in May. Hardening off simply involves putting them outside in the daytime and bringing indoors at night. Deep-green Black Beauty or yellow Goldrush are prolific. The speedy growth of a courgette can be truly amazing. 'Jets' are best picked small and taste lovely stir-fried, grated raw or lightly steamed.

The beetroot is one of many gastronomically important vegetables descended from *Beta vulgaris*, also known as the sea-beet. It is native to Western and Southern European coastlines from Sweden to the Mediterranean. This is believed to include Britain, although it's not until 1629 that the sea-beet is recorded in England. Selective breeding in the 1500's produced the familiar swollen-rooted crop. By the 1700's beetroot was popular fare at European mealtimes.

Full of natural sugars, beetroots are sweeter than the average vegetable. Their consumption is thought to promote relaxation and a general sense of well-being. In recent years supposed aphrodisiac qualities have been much vaulted.

HOEING, ROOT VEG AND RUNNER BEANS

April, 4th Week

Keep your hoe busy!
A dry spell at this time of year means perfect hoeing weather. Get busy with your hoe as early in the day as possible, to give sunshine plenty of time to shrivel up the annihilated weeds. Aim to pass the blade back and forth through the top layer of soil with small, smooth strokes. Keep the blade sharp with a small file which you carry in a pocket. Stopping regularly to keep your blade keen also affords an opportunity to stretch your back.

The hoe is a wildlife-friendly gardeners' number one ally in the battle with weeds from now and throughout the summer. Hoe when it is sunny, dry, and before you can see the weeds. I love getting in amongst my crops and having a really close, careful look at them.

Planting runner beans
Runner beans can be sown now. Enorma is high yielding with long, straight beans of excellent flavour. White Emergo is an old-fashioned, white flowered variety. It is prolific and tasty, as well as looking beautiful when in flower.

Pop the classic pink and white speckled beans 4 cm deep and on their ends, into small pots of compost. These are placed in the greenhouse or on a sunny windowsill and watered. Kept moist, they should start to sprout in a few days. Don't consider planting them outside until after all reasonable risk of frost has passed. Runners are very tender and easily killed by a late chill.

Root veg management
Parsnips, sown in mid-March, are just beginning to show their first pair of small pale-green leaves. It is a hard job spotting them

NATURAL HISTORY IN THE GARDEN
Cow Parsley

Cow parsley will be growing well this month. Its fern-like foliage bursts out from around the bases of trees, under hedges, and throughout areas of rough ground. As April passes, look out for the frothy flowers that reach up beyond the green leaves and dance atop them like a white mist. Each big flat platter of flowers is made up of half a dozen or more smaller flower heads, and each one of these consists of tiny individual florets.

amongst the seedling weeds at this stage, but I always make an effort to clear around the tiny 'snips when they first emerge. It's a painstaking job but well worth doing before the parsnip bed turns into a mini-jungle.

Thin salsify and scorzonera, which were sown earlier this month too. They germinate quickly. By now seedlings look like strands of grass. The weakest ones should be pulled from each sowing station, the lines weeded then watered.

VEGETABLE SNIPPETS
CATCH CROPS

Catch crop is the term used to describe a rapidly maturing crop that can be sown at the same time as another, longer term, main crop, with the seeds of both mixed together. The two grow cheek-by-jowl but being much faster of growth, the catch crop is harvested and eaten way in advance of the main crop. Having become established, the remaining developing plants then have plenty of room in which to thrive and plump up.

To this end, salsify and scorzonera seeds can be comfortably mixed with those of lettuces or radishes, which are ideal catch crops. They won't impede the root veggies, which will occupy the ground for many months, but will increase the yield and variety of foodstuffs which any one piece of ground can produce.

SWEDES

This is the perfect time of year for planting swedes. Marian is a great disease-resistant variety to try. I like to sow my swedes in between rows of winter Radar onions. These are pretty well grown by now and will be harvested in June. The thick green onion tops provide good protection for the germinating swedes, and a sowing in early May will have a month or so to sprout and be thinned before the seedlings are exposed to the elements, and pigeons. These birds love swede tops. Once the onions are gone, you can try to stop them from damaging your crops by running string between supporting posts to create a cobweb effect. This is thin enough to allow access to step in and weed, but thick enough to foil a landing pigeons' outstretched wings. Try also tying take-away cartons to sticks for the purpose of bird-scaring.

Sowing

Having thoroughly weeded the onions, 'station sow' swede seeds three at a time, 2 cm deep and 15 cm apart. Kept moist and with plenty of warm sunshine, they should be ready for thinning to the strongest seedling in twenty days or so. Further

NATURAL HISTORY IN THE GARDEN
Stinging Nettle

After April showers come May flowers. A vast array of common yet fascinating plants can transform the garden into a colourful wonderland this month. The stinging nettle grows abundantly in and around human habitation, and has done so for centuries. It thrives in the rich soils that are invariably created near where folk live. The 'stinger' is covered with tiny hairs all over. Even the faintest of touches will break the tips of these hairs and release a potent acid which is both painful and can cause a rash. However it is an important food source for many beautiful species of butterfly when in their caterpillar form, and people have used nettles through the ages for cloth, food and medicine. The delicious young tips can be pinched out and eaten. The sting is rendered harmless through steaming.

thinning will be needed in a few weeks to allow 30 cm between plants.

Swedes grow vigorously. They will swell up and, with luck, should provide a heavy yield of cream and purple-skinned, deep yellow-fleshed roots that are ready for harvesting from October onwards. Swedes are very hardy vegetables and can be left in the ground until needed in the kitchen.

VEGETABLE SNIPPETS
A BRIEF HISTORY OF
THE SWEDE

The swede (*Brassica napus*) is alternatively known to Americans as 'rutabaga' and to the Scots as 'neeps'. In northern England it is rather confusingly referred to as 'turnip'.

Some sources locate the development of swedes to seventeenth century Bohemia, where it was described as a cross between a cabbage and a turnip. By 1664 this vegetable was being cultivated in Britain and was popular across the colder northern European countries where it does well. Relatively easy to grow and hardy, swedes were an important staple of the war-time diet between 1939 and 1945 and are rich in vitamin A. The young leaves also make a hearty meal when taken and treated as for cabbage.

A WORD FROM THE FLOWER GARDEN

May, 2nd Week

This week my wife has been tidying up the long sprawling remains of her daffodils in the ornamental borders. In their full splendour the various varieties have sung the song of spring, and made the walk to my vegetable patch a true delight. However there is little more displeasing to her eye than that which is left behind, deflecting from the glory of the bluebells and shading shoots of irises yet to come into their own.

The challenge for my Lovely Lady is to fold and gently tie without using any string or bruising the leaves. It is tempting to cut them away, especially of the larger varieties, but beware! Such a measure may provide instant neatness but the bulb (and subsequently, next seasons produce) will not thank you for the lack of essential nutrients and goodness that it needs to re-absorb to thrive year after year.

Allowing time for the foliage to soften, my Sweetheart divides each group of stems and leaves and folds them either twice or thrice, using a couple of the softest outer leaves as ties to hold them in place. It is a skill that may take some practice, but be patient. Next spring your garden will repay you with a reward of golden delight.

NATURAL HISTORY IN THE GARDEN
White Dead-Nettle

The white dead-nettle looks similar to the stinger at first glance but is actually quite different. It is a member of the mint family. This month it sports clusters of white, hooded, flask-like flowers up the stem. It is much sought after by bumble bees and has adapted its flowers especially for them. When the bee dips down into the depths of the flower for a sip of nectar, pollen is brushed onto the fluffy insect's back by stamens (the male parts) which are concealed beneath the hood. As the bee works amongst other dead-nettles, it mixes pollen from different flowers onto the styles (female parts) of others, so ensuring that pollination occurs.

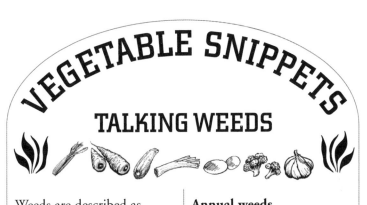

VEGETABLE SNIPPETS

TALKING WEEDS

Weeds are described as ephemeral, annual or perennial.

Ephemeral weeds

Ephemeral weeds are very short-lived and sometimes called 'ruderals'. These pioneering plants are amongst the first to colonise open soil. They can complete their life cycle in any month of the year, often producing several generations in one season. For example, chickweed can flower and set seed every five to six weeks, spawning on average 2,500 seeds per plant. Hairy bitter cress and groundsel are similarly short-lived and rapid reproducers, spilling an average of 600 and 1,500 seeds respectively every few weeks. All these ruderals are especially prolific in the months between April and October.

Annual weeds

Annual weeds cannot survive the cold of UK winters. They are adapted to grow, set seed and die over the course of one season. Wild flowers such as poppies, fat hen (Good King Henry) and cleavers (also known as 'sticky-buds', or 'goose grass') are examples of annuals. They over-winter as seeds which are produced in abundance.

Perennials

Perennials persist from year to year. Slower growing than the other types of weed, species such as dandelion and dock survive the winter cold and summer heat thanks to their thick, fleshy roots in which they gather and store reserves of nutrients and moisture. The daisy, so common and lovely in the lawn, is a perennial flower that stashes winter supplies in fibrous roots.

TURNIPS AND RUNNERS

May, 3rd Week

Turnips

Turnips of the F1 Market Express variety were sown in trays in the greenhouse around mid-February and then planted outside a month later. Now, over the last few days, the golf-ball sized roots, slightly conical and creamy coloured with a pinky-purple top, have all been pulled and eaten. F1 Market Express is an extremely fast growing 'nip which can be ready for harvesting and eating fifty days or so after sowing.

Succession sowing

For a succession of crops I suggest sowing turnips in short lines every couple of weeks until June. Rake the seed-bed into a fine tilth and sow the round, brown seeds, each the size of a pinhead, thinly and direct into a 2 cm deep drill. 'Nips like plenty to drink so keep them well watered. When the seedlings have appeared, thin them out to final spacings of 8 cm to afford them room to swell. Pigeons are partial to turnip tops so always protect them with twigs or wire netting.

Planting runner beans in the open air

My runner beans have been planted out this week too. They've come on well in

their pots and are showing two pairs of leaves. Runners can be grown up canes positioned 20 cm apart in wigwams, rows or against a south-west facing fence. The ground was prepared early in the year by trench composting. This involved almost filling the

NATURAL HISTORY IN THE GARDEN
Badgers in May

Badger cubs are now emerging from their setts with increasing confidence. As they explore this new world above ground the young badgers will be closely watched by their parents, in much the same way as mums keep an eye on toddlers playing in the garden.

dug-out growing area with kitchen and garden waste then topping up with soil. Hopefully this goodness in the ground will feed the hungry bean plants and encourage a bumper harvest. They'll need some training until they get themselves wrapped around the canes, but there is little else to do now except keep moist, weed-free and wait with eager anticipation.

Frost precautions
Having a fleece handy, ready to throw over the beans (or hardening-off courgettes) if there is a risk of a late frost could save a tender crop.

VEGETABLE SNIPPETS
SOME FACTS ABOUT
TURNIPS

Humans have cultivated turnips for thousands of years on account of the plump, edible, swollen stalk (not actually a root at all) which makes such good eating. They've been a feature of the European diet since Neolithic times, some 3000 BC. In the East wild turnips are recorded as being raised as a crop in India since 1500 BC. The seeds were pressed to produce cooking oil. Ancient Greeks and Romans enjoyed the culinary virtues of this plant too.

Turnips grow well in temperate climates across the world, and in northern Europe were a staple foodstuff of the poor until the 1500s when potatoes arrived from the Americas. In the 1800s what is now central London was a sea of veg. Turnips were intensively raised in the market gardens of the area at that time.

COURGETTES, NETTLES AND COMFREY

May, 4th Week

Planting out courgettes

When young courgette plants are filling their 8 cm pots and showing three or four true leaves, the time is right to plant them into the soil. Put them outside for a few days beforehand with protection at night to acclimatise them.

Plant courgettes in holes 60 cm apart with a dollop of compost at the bottom. Carefully hold the pots with your fingers supporting the stem at pot-rim level, and turn them upside-down. A couple of taps on the bottom releases the plant. The root-balls can be popped easily into the holes. Firm the soil around each one, gently.

Watering

These are thirsty plants. To make watering easier and less wasteful, earth-up a little ridge of soil to form a ring around each courgette plant. This stops water from running away and is especially helpful if the vegetables are grown on sloping ground. Water the soil not the leaves.

Home made fertiliser

An old wormery or compost bin with a tap can be regularly topped up with freshly cut stinging nettle and comfrey leaves. As these ferment within, the resulting juice they produce gathers at the bottom. This is a highly potent and traditional plant food. The concentrate is strained off as and when needed. A cupful stirred into a large watering can will be a real boost for those newly planted out courgettes.

Give all your veg regular nettle and comfrey feeds once they are past the tender seedling stage.

NATURAL HISTORY IN THE GARDEN
Leaves

Everywhere is turning different shades of green as buds burst out on trees. Leaves unfold and stretch themselves. Each is like an individual solar panel, absorbing sunlight energy and using it to convert carbon dioxide in air and water into growth-enabling carbohydrates. This is a process called photosynthesis and the by-product is oxygen, which is essential to life itself.

VEGETABLE SNIPPETS

MORE ABOUT COMFREY

'Bocking 14' is a sterile form of comfrey. As it does not go to seed there is no risk of it spreading wildly and taking over the veg plot. However it regenerates easily from portions of root. Care must be exercised to avoid spreading fragments to places where they are not wanted (the compost heap, for example) when digging in the area of this plant.

Comfrey concentrate is especially high in potassium (K). This important nutrient is an essential ingredient for veggies that flower, set seed, or fruit, such as tomatoes and courgettes. Farmyard manure (FYM) is an alternative source of K but comfrey is much richer, two or three times so. One reason for this is that the extensive roots plunge down deep into the soil and can access nutrient reserves which would otherwise be out of bounds. Dredged up thus, goodness is transferred into the foliage and is then made available in the soil when the leaves decompose.

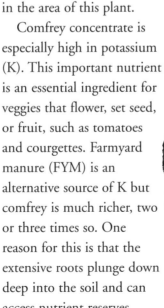

PURPLE SPROUTING BROCCOLI AND BROAD BEANS

Purple sprouting, steamed and served up in the spring or early summer with a knob of margarine melted over, is a food experience which we all wait for eagerly each year. In order to enjoy this seasonal pleasure, plant out young purple sprouting specimens into their final growing positions this week. They started life as pin-head sized brown seeds, popped into 7.5 cm pots of moist compost in the greenhouse around mid-April. It is a bit late to sow from seed now but seedlings are often available at markets and plant sales.

Preparing the ground

Dig over your bed and weed it thoroughly. Then tread the soil down to a firm surface with small sideways footsteps back and forth. Young plants can then put into the soil with 60 cm between them. Dig a hole with a trowel and lower the plants down. Fill the hole with water at this stage and wait for it to be absorbed before carefully filling in with soil and firming. Ensure that plants are deep enough so that the seed leaves, if they have not already turned yellow and dropped off, are either buried or at soil level.

Avoiding pests

Cabbage root fly is a danger to the transplants at this stage. They like to lay their eggs around the base of any brassicas. The hatching maggots burrow down to the roots where they settle and feed. The plant is either killed or weakened to the point of being useless. In order to prevent this from happening fit small collars around each plant base. Make them from carpet underlay cut into 10 cm squares, with a long slit to slide in snugly but not too tightly.

Pigeons are kept off with

NATURAL HISTORY IN THE GARDEN
Cuckoo in the Nest

The female cuckoo will be busy from the end of May. She seeks out the nests of small birds and, when the coast is clear, will fly down to eject one of the eggs. This is replaced with one of her own which is incubated, hatched and raised by the unknowing host. Mrs Cuckoo might lay up to a dozen eggs in a dozen different nests.

May, 5th Week

string stretched between sticks in a criss-cross fashion, and plastic bags tied onto canes. Keep a close eye on your purple sprouting and, all being well, you should be cutting the unopened flower heads in about 9 months' time.

Boosting a crop of broad beans

Broad beans which were planted in the first week of March are now flowering in profusion. Each flower is potentially a full pod of beans. Giving your broads plenty of water at this flowering stage will help the crop to fatten up nicely.

VEGETABLE SNIPPETS
CABBAGE ROOT FLY

The cabbage root fly is called *Delia radicum*. Adults on the wing are rarely noticed but their effects are a highly visible and upsetting feature in the cabbage patch every year, despite precautions. All members of the brassica family, including swedes, kale and Brussels sprouts, may be selected as fodder for their grubs. Affected plants fail to grow properly and have a listless, wilted appearance. At this point even a gentle tug will unearth a rotten stump where a mass of strong roots should be. The plant is fit only for burning. A peppering of white maggots on this stump, or in the immediately adjacent soil, reveals the culprits.

There may be three generations of this common garden pest wreaking havoc on the plot between spring and autumn. Females scout for suitable food plants, which may also include ornamentals such as wallflowers. Seedlings or fresh transplants are her preferred option. Once located, she lays her eggs on the soil surface around the stem. These hatch in due course, whereupon they burrow down and start munching. If left undisturbed, they will pupate (change into adults) underground and emerge to perpetuate the damage. Closely fitted collars of carpet underlay act as a physical barrier. The eggs are prevented from reaching the soil. They dry up and perish instead of hatching.

BLACKFLY ON BROAD BEANS

June, 1st Week

Blackfly can completely devastate a crop of broad beans at this time of year. They are the great enemy of broads. At flowering time masses of these irritating sap-sucking pests can descend on a crop and extract the life out of the beans as they form. It does not happen every year, but having suffered such heartbreak, I do try a number of ways to avoid this problem.

In years when blackfly is rife, pinch out the growing tips of your plants and burn them. This removes the most tender bit which the blackfly like best. For other affected areas, make up a weak washing-up liquid and water dilution and dispense this with a hand-held mist sprayer. Do this on a daily basis if you can, but it is not always satisfactory. Perhaps the most successful tactic to beat blackfly is to sow broad beans direct into the ground during November. This way a variety such as Aquadulce will grow on slowly throughout the winter months and produce pods for picking a fortnight or so earlier than a spring-sown crop.

The important thing is that autumn-sown broads are usually productive before blackfly are a problem. If they do clash, the advanced state of growth renders these broads more able to withstand attack.

In some years I've had to write off my spring-sown Witkiem. All is not lost however, as elsewhere on the veg plot Aquadulce was already feeding the family and there was hardly a blackfly in sight.

NATURAL HISTORY IN THE GARDEN
Cuckoo spit

Dripping globs of frothy spittle appear on grasses and plant stems all over the garden in June. Known as 'cuckoo spit', it is actually the work of an insect called the common froghopper. These sap-sucking bugs are mottled in their adult form, but the cuckoo spit hides and protects their tiny green larvae. The mass of bubbly goo is exuded from the anus of the juvenile froghopper.

VEGETABLE SNIPPETS
THE FASCINATING WORLD OF APHIDS

Aphids are also known as blackfly. They're a major pest of both farmer's field and kitchen garden but are also amazing creatures in their own right. They provide a major source of sustenance for useful species such as ladybirds, lacewings and hoverflies. Insect eating birds like blue tits may depend on them in hard times during winter, when they flock to the hedgerows and shrub borders, acrobatically ekeing out a meagre ration. Ants 'farm' them, protecting vast herds on the stems and underside of leaves. Using their antennae to stroke their charges, the ants receive a sugar-loaded drink of honeydew direct from the aphid's anus.

'Honeydew' is the sap which constantly flows around a plant. It is accessed by the aphid via its needle-like mouthpart, a hollow tube that is thrust into the tender host. Viruses are often transmitted from plant-to-plant by dirty 'needles'. Honeydew is rich in sugar and low in protein. In order to achieve satisfaction, enormous amounts must be consumed. Happily for the insects, it circulates at such a rapid rate that it is constantly dripping out of the feeding hordes. This is why plant foliage is often sticky in the summer, especially on trees like sycamore, and can be the cause of mouldy fungal growth later on. Weakened by these mass gatherings, infested plants often appear weakened and twisted.

In mild winters aphids may pass the coldest months as adults feeding amongst plot-side weeds. More usually, however, they over-winter as eggs. Spindle is a favourite host plant but ornamental lilacs and *Vibernum* species are also popular. In spring aphid 'nymphs' are born as already-pregnant females. This is called 'parthenogenesis' (virgin birth). A fortnight or so later, winged youngsters are being brought forth too. These take to the wing and find other host plants for a summer of feasting.

Aphids can be found in profusion on spinach, wild flowers such as thistles, poppies, dock, cultivated domestic roses and many other herbaceous plants. As the season turns towards autumn the bugs respond to decreasing daylight hours and temperatures by bearing winged males and females. They fly off, mate, and deposit eggs on a suitable host, whereby the cycle of life, death and rebirth continues for another year.

PLANTING OUT LEEKS

June, 2nd Week

You should be planting out your first batch of leeks into the main bed this week. Try growing a number of varieties to crop from September through to March. The tall, strong, long-shafted Axima will be harvestable well before New Year. Then the thicker, heavier Giant Winter variety will supply the kitchen until spring. Carentan 2 is an autumn cropping leek which I grow to eat as baby leeks in July. Mammoth can grow to be the size of a person's arm and will take some eating. I'm cultivating a few of these as a novelty.

Planting depth and distances

Sow the small black seeds in trays indoors from February to early April. Then transplant into a nursery bed when they're like blades of grass. When leeks are the size of pencils the time is right time to get them into their final growing positions. Dig the bed over and weed it thoroughly before sprinkling wood ash over it and raking to a fine tilth. Plant early leeks at 15 cm intervals in rows set 30 cm apart. Use a broken spade handle with a rounded-off end to push into the soil to a depth of 15 cm. Then pop the seedling leeks into these, one to a hole.

Essential watering

Next, puddle them in. This involves filling each hole with water. As it soaks in the roots will settle

NATURAL HISTORY IN THE GARDEN
Badgers in June

This is a month of plenty for badgers. Although classified as carnivores, badgers will in fact eat almost anything and they have a sweet tooth (they are 'omnivores'). Household scraps and kitchen waste are popular around human dwellings, as well as beetles, grubs, roots, bulbs and sweet veggies such as carrots. Young rabbits and moles will be dug out and dined upon, if available. Fruit becomes a major portion of their diet later in the year. Wasp and bee nests built into the ground are much sought after. But a badger's food of choice is the humble earthworm, which is sucked up like a string of spaghetti.

VEGETABLE SNIPPETS
NURSERY BEDS

down. Careful puddling-in daily for a week or so will be worth the effort because leeks respond well to generous watering at this stage. Later-maturing varieties can be planted out similarly in a fortnight or so at 20 cm intervals, except Carentan 2 which go directly from the nursery bed into the kitchen.

Future management
All that leeks require from now on is to be kept moist and weed-free.

'Nursery beds' bridge the gap between seedling and developing young adult. They are areas of the veg patch set aside for nursing seedlings through from pricking-out from trays to planting-out in the main plot. Hardy crops like leeks and brassicas (the 'cabbage tribe') are classic benefactors from this system of husbandry, where small plants can be lovingly nurtured through their tenderest stages under a close and watchful eye.

A high density of veggies can be cultivated in this small area, with careful attention paid to weed control and watering. In many respects this process is like potting-on into a larger container (which is a method I'll use to bring on courgettes and squashes before nestling them into the ground as soon as the risk of frost has passed).

Handling at all times must be with a deft touch. Seedlings are especially vulnerable to damage and bruising. Light manoeuvring, only holding the leaves, is essential. Roots should be kept as intact as possible. By the time they're ready to move on they should be tough little customers. None-the-less, a considered fork must be skilfully employed to loosen and lift the roots. With leeks, I suggest gathering them up in bunches and wrapping your charges in damp newspaper whilst out of the ground between nursery and main bed.

KOHLRABI

June, 3rd Week

This week I'll be sowing kohlrabi. This unusual-looking plant is a member of the cabbage family and is also known as 'turnip-rooted cabbage'. It is a quick growing green veg which has a swollen stem base with leaves growing from bracts around the middle and a tuft on top. The leaves are discarded in the kitchen and the bulbous part eaten. It is delicious steamed, sautéd or eaten raw either grated or cut into thin slices.

Sowing seeds

Delikatess is a reliable variety but there are others, even purple ones. Sow seeds thinly, 1.5 cm deep in a shallow drill. Shallow sowing is important to allow the stem bases room to swell. If sowing more than one row, space them 30 cm apart. As the seedlings grow and develop true leaves, thin them to allow 15 cm between individuals. Larger spacing can produce bigger crops but kohlrabi is at its best when the bulbs are not much bigger than a golf ball. It copes with dry conditions better than most veg although consistently giving them extra water can make them all the more tender.

You could now be pulling kohlrabi sown in March and looking forward to a late summer harvest from this week's sowing. A further line or two put down at the end of July should supply the kitchen into winter. Kohlrabi is hardy enough to stand in the ground until needed.

NATURAL HISTORY IN THE GARDEN
Wolf Spider

A compact spider which is commonly found scurrying around on bare earth or amongst low-growing plants such as speedwell is the wolf spider. This spider does not make a web. Instead, it catches its prey by running it into submission. Female wolf spiders carry their eggs around in a silken ball held close to their bodies and are easily recognisable by this habit. Several species of wolf spider even allow the young spiderlings to hitch a lift on their backs for a week or more after hatching.

VEGETABLE SNIPPETS

SOME FACTS ABOUT
KOHLRABI

This unusual looking brassica takes its name from the German *kohl*, meaning 'cabbage', and *rabi*, which means 'turnip'. Scientifically known as *Brassica oleracea va. caulo-rapa*, it was developed by selective breeding as a food crop in northern Europe during the 15th and 16th centuries. By the late 1700s, kohlrabi was being cultivated in Britain. Although not commonly consumed on these shores it is popular fare today in continental Europe.

POTTERING, TENDING RUNNER BEANS, JERUSALEM ARTICHOKES AND COURGETTES

By the end of June one might be enjoying finding the time to potter around. There is a definite lull in the vegetable garden now that the rush of spring planting is over and crops are harvestable all over the place. By sowing seeds of different crops a little and often you can ensure having lettuces, turnips, radishes, beetroot, kohlrabi and others at different stages of growth from seedling onwards. This 'succession-sowing' avoids a wasteful glut and ensures that there is fresh veg in the ground ripening over the whole summer.

Runner bean care

Runner beans should have grown to the top of their supporting canes. This is the time to pinch the growing tip out, to concentrate the bean's energy into flower production. Even if it has rained a lot they benefit from a good daily watering. Once in flower, add a splosh of nettle-and-comfrey concentrate to the watering can every two or three days.

How to manage Jerusalem artichokes in mid-summer

Cut about 45 cm off the top of your Jerusalem artichokes. They'll have grown thick, tall, leafy tops since being planted early in the year. They're quite susceptible to wind damage during summer storms so reducing their height now will lessen the risk of snapping.

NATURAL HISTORY IN THE GARDEN
House martins

House martins

Similar to swifts, but smaller and more fluttery in flight, are house martins. Viewed from the ground they appear black and white in colour, with shorter wings and a distinctive V-tail. House martins fly fast too, wheeling and twisting, arching and curling in the air. They trawl the skies for food with their mouths wide open, resembling penguins diving for fish in another element.

These birds make their nests close to people, in an enclosed cup-shaped nest tucked under house eaves. Martins are top-notch builders and construct their breeding chamber out of stuck-together balls of mud. However, too much tidiness

June, 4th Week

Lavishing love on your courgettes

When courgettes are beginning to fruit put a straw mulch around the plants. This has the dual purpose of conserving moisture, which courgettes suck up with great gusto, as well as keeping the rapidly forming and prolific fruits clean off the soil. The risk of blossom-end rot and slug damage is thus reduced. During any dry spell keep busy with your hoe. Fewer weeds means more space and goodness for the veg!

in the countryside and a dry spell in late spring can be disastrous for them because they need to locate mud of just the right texture from pond margins and dirty farmyards.

VEGETABLE SNIPPETS
MORE ABOUT WEEDS

A weed can be defined as a plant of any kind which is growing in the wrong place. There are many examples of this situation including chickweed smothering lettuces, moss in the lawn and last year's spuds in amongst current crops such as leaf beet. All weeds compete with cultivated plants for the three essential requirements of life: water, nutrients, light.

Some have what is called 'allelopathic' (poisonous) tendencies. The roots of such species produce chemicals that inhibit either the germination, growth or development of their neighbours. This can include veggies. Allelopathic plants include creeping buttercup, couch grass (sometimes called 'twitch'), creeping thistle and chickweed. Rhododendron is the classic poisonous plant. Introduced as cover for pheasants, it takes over large areas if left unchecked and is of poor wildlife value.

Pests and diseases can often be harboured on weeds. Fungal rust, an orangey powder that coats leaves, can affect garlic and leeks. It also thrives on groundsel, for instance. Fat hen (also known as Good King Henry) and dock frequently host vast armies of aphids which then home in on runner and broad bean crops.

CABBAGE WHITE BUTTERFLIES

We all hope to have some fine, healthy young specimens of purple sprouting broccoli by now. Planted out at the end of May, they stand around 30 cm in height with thick stems and juicy, broad leaves. Pigeons can be deterred by lines of string criss-crossing over them between sticks and, dangling on canes, take-away cartons that move and make a noise in the breeze. The big thing to look out for on all your brassicas from now onwards is butterfly damage. Two species lay their eggs on purple sprouting and other members of the cabbage tribe: the large and small white. They are on the wing now, sniffing out their favourite food-plants.

Large white

Large whites lay their tiny yellow eggs in clusters that are easy to detect on the underside of leaves. When the caterpillars hatch they eat their egg-cases and then start tucking into the leaf. At this stage they tend to feed together. As they grow they quickly spread out over the whole plant and can devastate it to the point of being a skeleton. The caterpillars are yellow and black.

Small white

The small white lays its minute eggs singly on the underside of the leaf. Its caterpillar is small and green. It takes some looking for. They are a particular problem on cabbages because they start feeding at the heart and then eat their way outwards.

NATURAL HISTORY IN THE GARDEN
Blackbirds

Keep an eye out for blackbirds congregating on the lawn this month, in groups of half a dozen or more. Members of the thrush family, the handsome males are glossy black with bright orange-yellow beaks and eye rings. Females are a duller brown.

Blackbirds like to hop, skip and jump over the turf, watching and listening for invertebrate movement. They'll stand still and cock their heads, keeping a keen ear out for the faint rustle of earthworm activity, before pouncing and stabbing the ground, then tugging out a tasty morsel. A blackbird whose beak is dripping full with worms may well be feeding a newly fledged youngster nearby.

VEGETABLE SNIPPETS

LARGE WHITE LIFE CYCLE

Chemical-free control

I make time at least twice a week to have a thorough hands-on check of my brassicas. I'll gently rub out patches of eggs with my thumb but prefer not to squash the caterpillars once they've hatched. Instead, use a fine paintbrush to remove them into a jar and relocate them elsewhere in the garden. These caterpillars love nasturtiums. Try growing some specifically for them.

Although it's a time consuming task, I get real pleasure from being outside looking for caterpillars and listening to birdsong on a peaceful summer evening.

Clouds of white butterflies mixing together above the cabbage patch, rising and falling in delicate dance like bubbles of fizz in a glass of lemonade, used to be a far more common sight in our towns and gardens before the widespread use of insecticides put paid to vast numbers of these infuriating but beautiful insects. In the vicinity of suitable food-plants where chemicals are shunned the wildlife-friendly grower may be treated to the spectacle of a gathered knot or three of these charming customers, bobbing and weaving as they pass across his or her little piece of Heaven, doing what they've always done, lending a delicious 'scene from yester-year' taste to the garden landscape.

They're amazing creatures. Large white adults are on the wing in April and May. Having survived the winter as a pupa tucked away somewhere sheltered and safe, they mate. She lays batches of yellow eggs on the underside of brassica leaves. In two weeks a mass of tiny caterpillars emerge with only one thing on their minds - to eat! This they do non-stop through June, growing quite large and distinctive.

When ready, the satiated caterpillars sneak away and hole-up in a handy crevice or woody cabbage stalk, to pupate. Forming a chrysalis to protect themselves during this most incredible transformation, they completely re-arrange their bodies both inside and out, then emerge in July as the familiar 'cabbage white' to wreak more havoc on the veg plot. A second generation of youngsters may prove more damaging than the first. This lot generally over-winter in a chrysalis to commence the process again when early-summer next comes around.

Natural predators of the large white include starlings, which scoff lots of these pests as caterpillars, and wasps who snatch them as food for their grubs. Spiders also do a fine job of snaring the adults, paralysing them, and then sucking their bodily juices dry.

BULL-NECKED ONIONS AND THE LAST GLOBE ARTICHOKES

Bull-necked onions

I hope you're pleased with the progress of your onions. Sets were planted throughout March and the rows kept moist and weed-free since then. If, like me, you popped the acorn-sized onion sets in at 15 cm intervals they should have thrived in this space. My bulbs are now mostly 7–10 cm across, with the odd few coming in at over 12 cm!

Whenever an onion has bolted and pushed up a flower-head, I've pinched it off. These bolting onions are a nuisance because they become 'bull-necked' and won't be any good for storing over the winter. The bulbs develop a solid central core and thick, stiff, central stem. I've observed that Red Baron are more likely to bolt than the white varieties. Any bull-neckers can be left in the ground with the rest of the crop but because they won't keep, they are worth pulling as and when required for cooking or to liven up summer salads.

NATURAL HISTORY IN THE GARDEN
Orange Hawkweed

Catching the eye with a vibrant display of cheery flowers in the banks around about is the orange hawk-weed. It's a lovely little low grower that displays vividly every year and should be on show this month. Another name for it is 'Fox-and-Cubs' on account of the foxy coloured blooms and the way they form in grouped bunches on their stalks.

July, 2nd Week

Managing globe artichokes

If you have a couple of meal-sized flower buds remaining on the globe artichokes cut them within the next few days and enjoy the exquisite experience that eating these glorious immature flower heads provides. After that it might be wise to remove any other small buds. Such husbandry will concentrate all the plant's energy back into itself, in readiness for another (hopefully) fine crop next June and July.

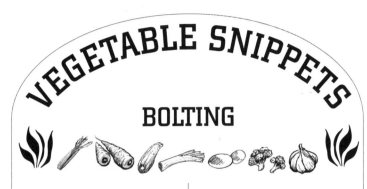

VEGETABLE SNIPPETS

BOLTING

Bolting is a phenomenon which occurs in 'biennial' plants. These are plants that grow for a season, rest (go dormant) for the winter, resume growth in the spring, then flower and set seed in the second summer. This includes onions, leeks and garlic, as well as many brassicas. Left to their own devices veggies like these will exhibit such behaviour.

Under normal circumstances the hungry gardener gets in there first and harvests the crops while still young and tender. However where the environment is harsh, due to weather extremes such as drought or frost, biennials can become stressed and produce flowers in their first year. This is 'bolting', and is a survival mechanism which has evolved as a way of securing the future of the species.

PERPETUAL SPINACH (LEAF BEET)

Perpetual spinach also goes under the name of 'leaf beet' which reflects the fact that it is not a member of the spinach family at all. It is closely related to beetroot but the leaves are very similar to spinach in taste. I grow leaf beet instead of spinach because I find it an easier and more reliable performer in the veg garden. It produces lovely big green leaves in profusion, and is far less prone to bolting during hot, dry spells. Sow leaf beet in March for cropping throughout the summer. Then, this week, sow another couple of 1.8 metre rows. Protect these later sowings throughout the winter under cloches and they should provide useful greens until the spring.

Sowing leaf beet

Leaf beet seeds are small and knobbly but large enough to handle individually. Sow them in a sunny bed, into soil that's been raked to a fine tilth. Sow seeds thinly in drills, not more than 1.5 cm deep and keep well watered. Allow 30 cm between rows. As the seedlings develop thin them out gradually. Aim for 20 cm spacings eventually.

Harvesting leaves

Care needs to be taken when the leaves are ready for eating. I prefer to cut them off as low down as possible with a sharp knife to avoid disturbing the roots, which can happen with heavy-handed

NATURAL HISTORY IN THE GARDEN
Yarrow

Yarrow is a plant which flowers this month. It can be seen in gardens or just beyond as an escapee, blooming in patches. It bears dense platters of white-petalled flowers with pale yellow centres. These are borne on stems rising out of thick, soft, slightly grey-green fern-like foliage. It's a deeply rooted, drought resistant member of the daisy family.

Anglo-Saxons referred to yarrow as 'woundwort', believing that a compress of yarrow and grease would heal puncture wounds and cuts. It was also picked and brought indoors to drive away evil and sickness. In olden times yarrow was thought to protect one's heart from being broken by a lover.

July, 3rd Week

snapping and tugging. Another plus for leaf beet is in the kitchen. Because the leaves grow upright from the ground and are not deeply ridged, they tend to be a lot less gritty than spinach. They are delicious steamed with or without the stalks, which take slightly longer to become tender.

VEGETABLE SNIPPETS
SOME FACTS ABOUT LEAF BEET

Perpetual spinach is a selectively bred descendant of the wild plant, sea beet, which is a coastal species. Sprawling and hairless, it blooms from summer to early autumn. The display is modest, with numerous small green and yellow flowers adorning a spike which issues forth centrally from a bunch of thick, fleshy, spatula-shaped, red-tinged, glossy leaves.

Cultivation and refining of the wild forerunner began way back in the Middle East some 2000 years ago. Perpetual spinach is a member of the 'goosefoot' family of plants, which have played an important role in human food production worldwide. Other goosefoots include Swiss chard, mangel-wurzels, and a range of fleshy-rooted beets.

Each seed may give rise to a cluster of seedlings because leaf-beet is 'multi-germ'. This means that contained within one seed is the potential to form many individuals. In the best interests of growing your own greens it is wise to let them all pop up and have a good examine whilst still tiny. The strongest most handsome specimen can then be selected at this stage as the plant to nurture and lavish with care and attention. Others may be carefully pinched or pulled out, with minimum disturbance to the roots of the one that will eventually be eaten.

LOTS OF BADGERS, BEETROOT, RUNNERS AND COURGETTES

Badger damage
Badgers can cause problems in high summer. With their naturally sweet tooth, they often take a shine to young parsnips. These loveable rogues dig neat holes and turf out the 10–13 cm long 'snips, nibble them and then leave them on the surface. A few 'snips get dragged to the edge of the plot and are eaten, with just the green tops discarded. It's upsetting to see lovingly tended crops vandalised like this. However it is an annual problem and one that won't go away. Badgers are persistent creatures of habit, enjoying carrots, sweet corn and all manner of soft fruit.

Taking precautions
As soon as they begin to lay into my crops I take what we call 'badger precautions'. This involves sinking jam jars into the soil amongst the veg and half-filling them with my own urine which is collected in a bucket. Most evenings for the next couple of months I'll take an evening stroll around the veggies and apply urine with a garden mist sprayer. Badgers are very shy of humans. The stinking liquid is an effective deterrent which is both free and limitless in supply.

How to keep runner beans producing
Runner beans should be producing pods in abundance now. Pick them daily before they become hard and stringy. This keeps runners in maximum cropping condition with lots of flowers and developing beans.

NATURAL HISTORY IN THE GARDEN
SWIFTS

As July presses relentlessly on, and with the school holidays upon us, a heatwave can inspire flocks of swifts to gather in the skies above the garden. As well as feeding on a wealth of insect life, young birds will be testing their wings and strengthening their lungs in preparation for a long migration back to over-wintering quarters in the Southern Hemisphere. They're a joy to watch on hot days, screaming and swooping, climbing and diving, like a shape-shifting shoal of sickle-shaped fish in the deep blue sky of an English summer.

July, 4th Week

Cutting and cooking courgettes

Courgettes are fruiting prolifically too. As with runners, the more you pick, the more they produce. Yellow Gold Rush and deep-green Black Beauty are very much on the menu at this time of year. Slicing them thinly and flash-frying in olive oil then seasoning with black pepper and a splash of soy sauce makes a delicious, quick and easy snack at any time of the day.

Beetroot in the kitchen

Beetroot are cropping thick and fast with plentiful supplies from now until autumn thanks to consistent succession sowing. In the kitchen, twist the leaves off about 2.5 cm up the stalk. This prevents all the lovely red juice from bleeding away whilst simmering to tenderness in the pot.

VEGETABLE SNIPPETS

BEETROOT RED

The vibrant 'beetroot-red' stain that is so characteristic of this vegetable is a purple pigment which exists within the plants cells. Cutting through the root with a sharp knife breaks the cells. The pigment floods out and is said to be 'bleeding'. This can occur inside the human body as well as on the chopping board, staining both solid and liquid waste as it passes through. It's perfectly normal and harmless although the visual effects can be alarming! It is not unheard of for paramedics to get an emergency call from worried patients who are experiencing nothing more serious than the colourful consequences of indulging in the consumption of this swollen root veg.

Nutritionally, beetroot is rich in dietary fibre, vitamin C and a number of minerals. The leaves, when steamed as for spinach, provide an excellent source of iron and calcium.

ONIONS, SPRING ONIONS AND JERUSALEM ARTICHOKES

When to harvest onions

As August arrives onions will be very much on my mind. The maincrops, Stuttgarter Giant, Sturon and Red Baron, should be fat and shiny in the ground. When their tops are turning brown and withering, don't worry. The bulbs should be ripening beautifully in the hot sun. Let onion tops die back naturally with the crop still in the ground. Bending over the tops carefully at the neck, if soft enough, is another way to expose the crop to the sun.

Harvesting will take place soon, with a watchful eye on the weather. If the forecast suggests it is set fine for some time at the end of August, a crop will be happy left in the ground. If wet weather threatens the latter half of the month, better to opt to lift onions and hang them in a sheltered but airy place, in bunches, to dry.

Sowing spring onions

Spring onions can still be sown. If you feel in the mood, get in a quick-growing variety such as Guardsman, which can be pulled for autumn salads in October or over-wintered with protection for a very early spring crop. Sow the pinhead-sized black seeds carefully, evenly and not too thickly, less than 1 cm deep with 10 cm between rows. I've found that emptying the seeds into the palm of one hand and sowing with thumb and fore-finger of the other is the easiest way.

At this time of year it is important to keep the germinating seeds moist. Grass-like shoots should appear within a few days.

NATURAL HISTORY IN THE GARDEN
Wood Pigeons

Look out for wood pigeons. These handsome, fat, grey and pink birds like to sit in large trees on a hot summer afternoon or evening, wheezily and endlessly repeating their 'coo-coo-coo-cu-coo' song. Every now and then a woodie, with a clap of wings, will launch itself into the air from the leafy canopy, swoop down, then fly up in an arc with wings outstretched. This up/flap, down/glide, undulating flight is typically circular and the pigeon returns from whence it came to continue its lazy calling.

August, 1st Week

Seasonal artichoke care
Jerusalem artichokes will have put on so much growth that you'll need to cut back the rampant top-growth again, by nearly a third. Do this because the thick bushy growth is prone to being rocked about in strong summer winds. Reducing the height a bit lessens the chances of serious wind damage.

VEGETABLE SNIPPETS
WILD ONIONS

The wild onion (*Allium vineale*) is alternatively known as 'crow garlic'. It's a persistent weed of English and Welsh grasslands. This plant is a tough little customer, identifiable by papery-sheathed flower heads which rise out of grass-like tufts of green leaves. Within this wrap, or 'spathe', are contained small, pale pink flowers and a cluster of rice-grain sized, pointy-ended bulbs. Each of these has the potential to break free, fall to earth and develop independently.

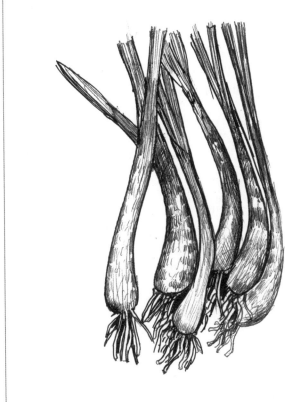

MOLES, MOLEHILLS AND WEEDING

August, 2nd Week

Saving your molehills

Moles are very busy at this time of year. Although their tunnelling can interfere with root crops, I generally welcome them. The soil which they push up into little mounds is of the finest quality: fresh, crumbly, and virtually weed-free. Why not do as I do and collect this molehill soil? Shovel it into old compost bags and store these in an out-of-the-way, shaded corner. Molehills are very useful for bulking-up potting compost. I use them in the spring for this purpose. Mixed molehills and leafmould also make a fine medium for growing-on seedlings.

Mole benefits and control

Moles do far more good than bad in the veg patch. They eat a lot of soil pests and their underground tunnels can assist with drainage in heavy soils. Moles can co-exist with surface-rooting crops such as beans and greens quite happily. However if moles do move into part of the veg patch where they are not welcome, such as a parsnip or asparagus bed, it might be sensible to move them on. To do this in a wildlife-friendly way, push freshly cut elder sticks and twigs into the molehills, and also any tunnels if they are visible close to the surface. This simple method proves effective time and time again although I can't explain why.

NATURAL HISTORY IN THE GARDEN
Wasps

Wasps have been spending most of the spring and early summer nest building and hunting out caterpillars and grubs to feed their larvae. In return, the larvae produce a sweet 'honeydew' for the workers to feed on. However at this time of year the queen winds down her egg laying so the wasps need to seek out alternative sources of sweet food. They are far more visible now as sugary drinks and snacks, taken into the garden to enjoy in the open air, become an alternative form of sustenance for them.

When being hassled by scavenging wasps, it is worth remembering that each colony of up to 2,000 individuals accounts for many thousands of insect pests every year.

Methods of weeding

The hoe should be kept busy annihilating weeds during dry spells. A useful tool for delicate hoeing in tight spaces is a dinner knife, with the blade bent at 90 degrees halfway along its length. Use it to slice the weeds off just below the soil surface with a controlled scraping motion. Use a hoe to weed between rows and a bent knife to get in between the individual plants.

When the soil is moist, most weeds will pull out whole with a bit of gentle persuasion. If the root is particularly deep, employ a hand-fork to loosen the soil just enough to tease the root out. I keep an old dinner-fork in my pocket too, for exactly the same purpose, when soil disturbance needs to be kept to a minimum.

VEGETABLE SNIPPETS
FARMYARD MANURE (FYM)

Farmyard manure (FYM) is quite possibly the best organic matter which vegetable growers can lay their hands on. In the olden times, when horsepower was the order of the day, it was widely and readily available. In 1950 as mechanisation kicked in after the Second World War, there were still 300,000 horses working on farms, according to government statistics. Nowadays a working horse is a novelty. FYM can be difficult to get hold of, but is well worth tracking down.

It has many virtues apart from being a slow-release fertiliser that contains all the essential nutrients demanded for healthy veg growth. The bulky nature of the stuff aids soil moisture retention. Healthy soil literally teems with life, and good old fashioned 'muck' is a dynamic improver of soil organism populations. FYM maintains and boosts the structure too, assisting with both breaking up heavy growing mediums and binding those which are light.

However a little care is a necessary precaution. Nutrient values can vary from load to load depending on the proportions of faeces, urine, straw and other bedding contained therein. FYM must also be well decomposed or else it can release ammonia and other toxic substances which are by-products given off by the army of microscopic creatures which are actively breaking it down. Lastly, FYM is dirty and heavy to handle so watch your back when loading and unloading.

STORING ONIONS AND SOWING GREEN MANURE

Storing onions

Onions are ripe for harvesting when the shiny bulbs with browned-off tops lift easily from the ground, and the roots are withered and dry. Sort your onions out before tying them in bunches and hanging them in a sheltered and airy place to dry completely. A few always come up soft and mushy. Put these straight onto the compost heap. Others might be soft and brownish under the papery skin around the neck and are liable to suffer 'neck rot' in store. Put them aside for consumption first with any that have bolted and have a thick, stiff central stem.

The vast majority will usually be fine and be ready to store for the winter in a frost-free shed, suspended from the beams. If you end up with more onions than can be comfortably hung, keep them one-deep in fruit trays. Stored this way after a good season, onions should last well into early next summer.

Sowing green manure

With large areas of the veg garden now becoming empty, 'green manure' crops can be sown. They're not grown for eating but to replenish or improve the soil. Green manures are usually hoed off and/or dug into the plot before they flower. I like to scatter seeds of *Phacelia* onto open ground at this time of year. It's a quick growing plant that will suppress weeds and can be dug in during the autumn or left to over-

NATURAL HISTORY IN THE GARDEN
Slow Worms

Slow worms are resident dwellers in and around the wilder, rougher parts of many veg plots. They may be chanced upon as they bask on the sun-kissed banks this month. In spite of their snake-like appearance slow worms are in fact legless lizards and totally harmless to humans.

A large specimen can be finger-thick and nearly 30 cm in length. Their skin is fairly uniform in colour, ranging from brown-gold through to silver-grey and, although made up of tiny scales, it is silky smooth to the touch. If startled, slow worms will glide effortlessly into the thick sward. From the moment they are born their favourite food is slugs which are consumed in vast quantities.

August, 3rd Week

winter. *Phacelia* is good because inevitably some will be missed and allowed to bloom. The delicate blue flowers start off like a tufted bud and then unfurl into a long tongue of tiny flowers which beneficial insects adore.

VEGETABLE SNIPPETS
MORE FACT ABOUT ONIONS

Gasses released by broken cells during the preparation of onions in the kitchen are the causes of crying at this time. Try chewing on a hunk of bread, without swallowing, to calm the stinging irritation. My mother employs this tactic when onions are on her chopping board and it works every time although she's not sure exactly how or why.

The potent and flavoursome layers which make up an onion are actually modified leaves in which the plant stores supplies of food and water to survive the winter. The stem of an onion is internal. It is that bit just above the roots from which the edible leaves arise.

In the agricultural depression from 1348 to 1500, caused when the black death wiped out nearly half of the entire UK population, onions were an important ingredient in stews cooked up by the poor folk of those Medieval times. Known as 'pottage', it included whatever veg could be grown in a small piece of land set aside for cultivating food, called a 'pottager'. According to the season, pottage typically consisted of onions, garlic, colewort, leeks, parley, scallions, carrot, parsnip, turnip, chervil, chives and rosemary.

FLOWERS IN THE VEG PATCH

August, 4th Week

Traditional agricultural flowers like poppies, corn cockle, cornflower, corn marigold and the wild pansy grew in vast numbers before the use of weed

killers became widespread. If given a chance they will still thrive on regularly disturbed land and are very at home growing in amongst vegetables. I love 'em and, although I do control them so they don't take over, I'll always allow a few personal favourites to bloom and set seed.

Harvesting wild flower seeds

This week is a good time for collecting the ripe seeds of corn cockle and wild pansy so you can sow them and grow them where you'd like them next year. Gather seeds during dry sunny weather, shaking them into

NATURAL HISTORY IN THE GARDEN

Badgers in August

At about 6 kg, badger cubs will have reached about half their adult weight by the beginning of this month. Badgers are often seen at night as they patrol the gardens and neighbourhood. Dry weather causes foraging further afield, while back at home they will be busy extending and renovating their setts.

paper bags. Wild flowers in the veg patch can be very pleasing to look at and will attract all sorts of bees and other useful insects. I'm convinced that growing wild flowers and veg together like this creates a healthy, naturally balanced environment.

Pot marigolds

The Calendula or pot marigold, which grows around the edges of my veg patch, are now thick with both flowers and ripe seeds. This plant is grown to stop encroaching couch grass, which cannot tolerate residing in amongst Calendula roots. I'll save a load in preparation for sowing next spring. This will not only keep the plot free of troublesome couch, but also save a packet on purchasing seeds.

VEGETABLE SNIPPETS
RED MASON BEE
(OSMIA RUFA)

The red mason bee, *Osmia rufa*, is a highly beneficial and hard-working insect. Crops that depend on flowering to produce a cache of nutritious food will be serviced by these fellows, from peas and beans through to all manner of lovely fruits.

Purpose-built nests are available from specialist firms and good garden centres. They consist of a plastic cylinder which contains cardboard straws, typically 30 or 100, and it is these that provide a potential nursery for the young bees. They imitate naturally occurring nesting sites which in the wild include hollow plant stems and beetle holes in wood.

Red mason bees are commonly seen in the vicinity of old walls and out-buildings, passing in and out of little holes in the masonry. However, contrary to popular belief, they are not responsible for excavating these cavities themselves. The mining work is largely done by the solitary, white-banded Davies' colletes, one of eight UK species of *colletes* bee.

The red masons simply clean out and renovate suitable sites in the crumbly mortar of old brick and stonework, where they lay their eggs in self-sufficient chambers which they construct (empty nail or vine-eye holes are other favourites).

Proprietary nests secured to a south- or west-facing fence or shed at or above chest height in early spring might attract mason and also leaf-cutter bees.

Red masons are busy in low temperatures when bumble bees hunker down and remain inactive. Their peak period for useful toil, as far as the home-producer is concerned, coincides with a wide range of top-fruit blossom (apples, pears, plums and the like), and one red mason is reputed to do the pollination work of 140 honey-bee workers. With no sting (they don't produce honey so have no need to defend their stores) they are safe and harmless around children and family areas in the garden.

ROOT VEG

August, 5th Week

Now's a good time to have a thorough weeding and tidying session in amongst the root veg. Get stuck in to it this week!

Parsnips

Parsnips should be making good growth. Hand weed and hoe through the crop, taking care not to damage the parsnip tops. Remove browned-off leaves and chuck them onto the compost heap. This not only keeps the crop clean but also removes slug and snail hidey-holes.

Swedes

By late August swedes will be fattening up. Some might assume cricket-ball sized proportions. The odd plant has not grown and the small roots have turned to mush. Whilst weeding in the swede bed take out all of these bad ones, as well as any yellowing leaves from others. Keeping the crop healthy in this way is an important tactic for maintaining the good swedes in peak condition. Being a member of the cabbage family, they are attractive to both the large and small white butterflies as food plants for their caterpillars. Crush the eggs and carefully remove caterpillars to nasturtiums grown as an alternative food plant elsewhere on the plot.

Scorzonera

Judging from the lush crowns of long, spatula-shaped leaves, the elongated thong-like roots of scorzonera should be going down deep. But some might be sending up flower spikes. Cut out these flowers. They resemble beautiful, ragged dandelion heads on 60 cm stalks. Sever them low down to concentrate the plant's energy into the roots.

NATURAL HISTORY IN THE GARDEN
House Martins

House martin numbers increase in August as fledglings take to the skies. Just sitting in the garden of a peaceful evening and gazing skywards provides stunning viewing of these lively, aerodynamic black and white birds. Their flight is both dashing and playful. Listen out for the house martins communicating with each other mid-flight, by way of a distinctive and friendly bubbling squeak.

Salsify

At this time of year, rows of salsify look similar to leeks. They are a highly rewarding, low maintenance crop. Their tussocks of grey-green leaves are so massed that they smother out most weeds. The odd rogue thistle can be teased out by hand, or chopped off with a long handled hoe.

Autumnal care

All these roots require little more than a watchful eye, and to be kept moist and weed-free throughout the coming autumn.

VEGETABLE SNIPPETS

OUT-OF-SEASON PARSNIPS

It's not just foraging badgers that like to enjoy parsnips out of season. The home-producer can, too. For something different at this time of year, and as a taste of things to come, lift a bunch or two for a roasted treat. To give them that special sweetness, which only comes as a result of the first hard winter frosts, pop the pale roots into your refrigerator for a couple or three days prior to cooking them up.

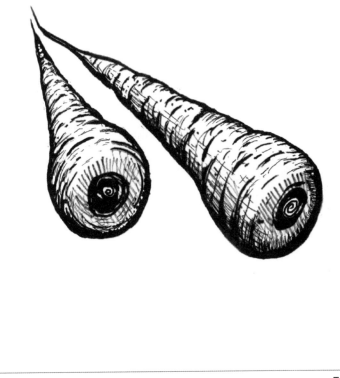

WINTER ONIONS

September, 1st Week

September is the month to plant winter onion sets. They are widely available and alternatively known as 'autumn onions'. You'll likely get consistently good returns with the Radar variety. They will tough out even the harshest winter, swell up in spring, and ripen for harvesting in late May. Winter onions do not store for very long, unlike maincrops, but are valuable in early summer when stored maincrop supplies are low or have been exhausted.

Preparing the ground

Onions like a sunny position and firm root-run. Prepare your onion bed a few days in advance of planting. Lightly fork over the selected plot and scatter handfuls of wood ash over it. Aim to dust the soil thinly but evenly. Rake the bed level and to a crumbly tilth, then tread it down again before raking some more. Plant the sets at 15 cm intervals with 30 cm between rows.

Planting

Straight rows are much easier to look after than wonky ones, so I'd advise using a line of string tied between two sticks to mark them out. Then make a little planting nest for each one with your finger so as not to damage the acorn-sized miniature onion as you push it into the soil. Employ both hands, using thumbs and first-finger knuckles to secure each set. But leave the top of the bulb exposed. Sprouting roots can lift them out if they are not nestled in snugly. There is little else to do apart from keeping moist and weed-free, watch and wait.

NATURAL HISTORY IN THE GARDEN
Slow Worm Babies

September is the prime month for slow worm babies to be born. Females hold their eggs internally until virtually the point of hatching, whereupon they deposit 6 to 12 fully developed youngsters in a thin, transparent shell that breaks open almost immediately. The 5 cm long, legless lizards are beautiful black and gold slivers of muscle the thickness of a knitting needle. Completely independent, they start feeding on tiny slugs straightaway.

VEGETABLE SNIPPETS
THE PROS AND CONS OF USING PEAT

For me, growing veg is about much more than just eating food. It's a wonderful thing to plant Radar onions in fabulous Indian summer weather as vast, shape-shifting gatherings of house martins and swallows work the insect-rich skies above. Being an active piece in the web of life and feeling in tune with the rhythm of the seasons is all part of the magic.

Peat is partially decomposed plant debris and is located in bogs and moors. These are basically cool, water-logged environments. Taking thousands of years to form, peat is arguably the best growing medium for cultivating seedlings of a wide range of plants. It is stable, long lasting, well aerated, moisture retentive and an extremely popular choice in the greenhouse or shed as potting compost.

However the peat industry for horticultural purposes has been responsible for the destruction of huge areas of British peat lands in the latter half of the 20th century. These areas are, coincidentally, home to a range of rare or specialised plants and animals which are threatened by this habitat loss: wildlife such as sundews, butterworts and bladderworts (all carnivorous plants), nightjars (summer visiting relatives of the woodpecker) and many species of weird and wonderful insects.

There is also a global warming issue linked with peat extraction. Being plant matter, a vast amount of carbon is locked up in peat. When it is removed and used, this carbon is released into the atmosphere which enhances the 'greenhouse effect'. The quantities of carbon contained herein, and potential damage caused by its liberation, should not be underesti-mated.

LEAFMOULD AND COMPOST

September, 2nd Week

Making cheap and easy bins

This is a good time of year to empty compost and leafmould bins. I make these containers cheaply and simply with old wooden pallets, set on end in a square and lashed together with strong wire. They're functional and well ventilated. Mine are adjacent to each other so they can be easily worked in tandem.

Leafmould

The leafmould is from last season's fall. Although not entirely broken down, it's rich, dark and crumbly – a lovely soil conditioner and good moisture retaining medium. I'm an avid leaf collector during the autumn months and will scavenge the fallen bounty from almost everywhere and anywhere, except the sides of busy roads and woodlands. Roadside leaves are liable to be polluted and are best left alone. Those falling in wooded areas should be respectfully passed over also. They are an important part of the woodland cycle of life and death.

Compost

The compost bin has been filled with everything green over the last couple of years except potatoes and tomatoes (which are prone to carrying diseases), and particularly invasive weeds such as horsetail, bindweed and couch grass. You'll be amazed to see how your compost heap can reduce from over-flowing to half-full in a matter of days.

NATURAL HISTORY IN THE GARDEN
Ivy-leaved Toadflax

Look out for a delightful little plant which adorns walls in the garden. It's called Ivy-leaved toadflax, a member of the figwort family that seeks a root-hold in cracks between stones and bricks. It tumbles out in straggly tufts. September is the end of a long flowering season which began in early summer. Ivy-leaved toadflax sports dainty pale purple flowers which are like miniature versions of the familiar garden snapdragon *Antirrinum* and, as the name suggests, has small ivy-shaped leaves. Once fertilised, this plant begins to physically curve its stems into the wall, pressing its tiny, ridged seeds into the cracks.

VEGETABLE SNIPPETS
SOME FACTS ABOUT LEAFMOULD

How to use them

I dig the leafmould out first and wheelbarrow it onto bare soil in the veg patch. The top of the compost heap, which has not yet rotted, is removed into this space when it is empty. Underneath is a sweet-smelling, fertile mixture which is ripe for depositing over the plot in piles also. As crops are cleared I'll cover bare soil with these home-made soil improving fertilisers and leave them until late winter. Then the whole lot can be dug in as preparation for another season of hopefully healthy and heavy-cropping home grown produce.

Unlike green garden waste, which relies heavily on micro-bacteria to break it down into a wonderfully earthy compost, leaves utilise the rotting powers of fungi. Hence, leafmould is longer in the making, generally speaking, than compost. A heap of decomposing leaves should not be allowed to dry out, so dousing it with water may be necessary during a dry summer.

Leafmould is of only limited benefit when it comes to boosting nutrients in the soil. Apart from maintaining and enhancing the structure of the growing medium, and also its moisture retaining properties, the main virtue of leafmould is the role it plays in encouraging soil life. The largely invisible (to the naked eye) hordes of swarming microscopic and minute animals and fungi are an absolutely essential component of a fully functioning, healthy garden ecosystem.

Two words of caution, however – partially decomposed leafmould can rob nitrogen from the soil, and pine needles are strongly acidic so best avoided on the veg patch.

This bulky organic material can be easily made on a small scale with plastic bin bags. Simply fill a bag with leaves during the autumn, tie together at the top, stab a few holes in the sides for ventilation and store out of the way somewhere. Forgotten about for a few months, the leaves will have transformed into a really useful mulch in a year or so.

WINTER PURSLANE AND CORN SALAD

September, 3rd Week

Winter purslane

Claytonia, or winter purslane, is a pretty little plant that will provide succulent fresh green leaves for use as a salad garnish during the winter months. Also known as 'miners' lettuce', in the past it was grown widely by working families as an important food source for when the days are short and the nights long.

Sowing in the greenhouse

Why not sow some of your own winter purslane this week? Sprinkle the shiny black pinhead-sized seeds over a tray of moist compost in much the same way as one might apply a pinch of salt to a plate of food. Barely cover them with a fine layer of compost. Seed trays could be put into the greenhouse to germinate but a cool windowsill is also ideal. The seeds require only to be kept moist and in good light. They should start showing tiny shoots in a few days. Grow on until large enough to handle then transplant outside in rows at 10 cm intervals.

Planting outside

Once in the open air these autumn-sown plants are most productive when given the protection of a cloche covering. Individual leaves can be picked as soon as they are large enough, about the size of a two-pence piece. White flowers stem from the centre of round leaves which resemble a belly-button. These are edible, too. Winter purslane develops into a compact, low rosette of leaves which thrives on regular pickings. A dozen or more plants should

NATURAL HISTORY IN THE GARDEN
Blackbirds and Elderberries

Elderberries are swelling in darkening, ripening bunches that drip from the branches of the bushes that are dotted over the bank which backs on to my plot. They're attractive to blackbirds. Flocks descend on the heavily laden plants this month. These handsome fellows like to cluck quietly to themselves as they gulp down a few berries, look up and around, shift position, and gobble up some more. Like most of the wildlife in the garden environment, the birds gorge themselves on nature's bounty during these heady days of plenty.

VEGETABLE SNIPPETS

SOME FACTS ABOUT WINTER PURSLANE AND CORN SALAD

provide sufficient greens to keep a family of four in fresh salad throughout the dark months.

Sowing corn salad

Corn salad, or lambs' lettuce, is another hardy vegetable which we can all grow for a winter garnish. Scatter, or 'broadcast sow', the small brown seeds on any spare patch of soil before raking them in. They'll develop happily enough with or without a cloche, producing stout little plants. Leaves can be picked individually but are a bit small. You might prefer to tease out plants, dunk them in water to wash, trim the root, and present whole on a plate or in sandwiches. Corn salad has a pleasant nutty flavour and self-sows freely if a few are left to flower. I've got it coming up, as if by magic, in various corners of the veg garden and it's always welcome.

Winter purslane

Winter purslane might be called 'miner's lettuce'. This name came about from the days of the American gold-rush. In those frantic and sometimes desperate times, the fleshy leaves provided miners for gold with a crucial source of vitamin C. They actually depended on this low-growing plant to ward off scurvy. It's a good crop to cultivate in a partially sheltered spot as this mimics its chosen natural habitat which would be shaded by trees.

Corn salad

Round about 1600 corn salad was introduced to the UK. It came from the Low Countries of northern Europe. The petite plant's alternative name, 'lambs' lettuce', refers to the fact that it is reputed to be at its greenest and most tender come the end of winter, which coincides with the traditional start of the lambing season.

As an escapee to the wild, in the UK it grows as a discreet plant that looks very much like a miniature forget-me-not. Corn salad prefers the dry soils provided by hedge banks and dunes. In places it may be a common weed of arable farmland.

RUNNERS, GREENS AND COMFREY

September, 4th Week

Runner beans

Runner beans have worked hard and consistently since July. They've responded to meticulous preparation and care magnificently but now are virtually spent. Fill a trug for the last time this week before consigning them to the compost heap.

Always snip the stem just above ground level because there is a lot of nitrogen goodness in bean roots that will be returned to the soil as they decompose. Canes can then be untied, pulled up, turned upside-down, and the whole 2 metres or more of runner bean stem and leaf are slipped off in one go. There are always fat pods of beans, drying and dried, hidden away. Some of these can be saved for sowing next year.

Leaf beet and Swiss chard

Strip your March-sown leaf beet and Swiss chard this week. Carefully pull the leaves, tugging downwards and sideways at once, or cut them with a sharp knife. Remove all the big tough outside leaves, leaving only a whorl of small, tender greenery. They should respond to this seemingly harsh treatment by growing more leaves for winter greens.

While the weather is mild, they can be left as they are. But before the first cold snap mulch them thickly with straw or dry bracken to keep them cosy.

Comfrey

Comfrey continues to grow in abundance. Cut it right back again and stuff the leaves into an old wormery bin. Keep on top of the nettles too, thus ensuring a regular flush of fresh nettle tops. These are also put into the old wormery. Reward for this work is the

NATURAL HISTORY IN THE GARDEN
Badgers in September

Badgers have had a busy month. They will have been fattening up for winter and high on their menu right now will be blackberries. This wild harvest grows abundantly all over. Finishing touches will be made to sett renovations or extensions. Dry grass and other vegetation is much sought after by badgers for bedding. They'll be collecting as much as they can to cosy-up their underground dwelling.

VEGETABLE SNIPPETS
AN EXPERIMENT WITH BEANS

potent liquid manure which will be strained off in early spring and used to feed all of next season's crops.

The difference between runner and French beans can be easily seen at seedling stage. In runners the bean splits open whereupon a shoot pushes up and out from within. The two bean halves are called 'cotyledons'. They are the embryonic first seed-leaves (not true leaves at all) and remain underground after germination. French beans develop differently at this stage. As they respond to moisture the cotyledons arch up and out of the soil on top of a root shoot then break apart to reveal the leaves inside.

Such quirks are easily demonstrated in a fun experiment for kids of all ages. By stuffing a jam jar full with damp (but not dripping) toilet paper or kitchen towels and pushing a mix of three or four beans halfway down the sides against the glass, their progress can be followed. Subtle differences in germination can be observed and noted by the youngsters. A simple activity like this is fun, educational, and can have the added bonus of inspiring a lifelong interest in growing plants for future generations of budding gardeners.

SORTING OUT THE SHED

Throughout the hectic months of summer a whole array of useful bits and bobs, and a fair portion of useless articles too, gets stashed in the shed. Why not get in there and have a jolly good sort out this week? It's a major job, one that should be tackled at least each spring and autumn. At this time of year it's prompted by the pressing need to create a handy space for stored potatoes, onions, squashes and other veg. These all need cool, frost-free conditions. You'll find the pleasure in cooking home-grown produce is increased enormously if you can nip out to the shed on a dark evening and lay your hands on what is wanted without fighting through a jungle of clutter first.

Personally, I find getting the shed in good working order calms my whole being. If something needs doing, I can get to it with minimum fuss when I know where to find the appropriate tool or piece of kit. Rolls of wire, off-cuts of fleece, ropes, netting, sieves, pots and trays, bubble wrap, cloches, glass jars, fertilisers, carpet underlay, plastic bags, water carrying vessels, endless lengths of string and twine, bamboo canes, old newspapers, hoses, clothes pegs, squeezy bottles and much more, all do important jobs in the veg garden. Aim to store everything in an accessible and obvious manner.

NATURAL HISTORY IN THE GARDEN
Garden Cross (Diadem) Spiders

There are lots of spiders about at this time of year. Orb-web spiders are very much in evidence. The Garden Cross, or 'diadem', is one of 40 different species in Britain. It is these little beasties that spin the classic webs which hang as if festooned with a thousand glistening pearls on a dewy autumn morning, suspended between the skeletal stems of tall herbs and grasses which the thoughtful gardener leaves uncut around the plot margins.

Such silken snares are mostly made by females, who wait patiently in the centre until the vibrations of a trapped insect spur her into action and she pounces. She injects her hapless prey with a poison that paralyses the victim, but does not kill it straightaway. Then she wraps it in a purse of silk which keeps it fresh until she is ready to suck the body juices dry.

'A place for everything, and everything in its place.' Then tools can be cleaned and hoes sharpened. Broken trowels and rakes may be put to one side for repair later. A drop of oil to the moving parts of shears and secateurs can rejuvenate them. Dried seeds of favourite flowers can be sorted into old margarine tubs and laid out on a surface for further attention another time. Keep the floor as clear as possible with workbench swept and ready for action.

I want my shed to be a quiet, peaceful oasis. I've a selection of choice reference books to dip in to plus next year's seed catalogues to study and plan from. Connecting an electricity supply is something that is well worth doing. The combination of light, power and order from chaos creates a beautiful space in which to potter away long evenings dreaming of what has been and what is to come.

VEGETABLE SNIPPETS
MULCHING IN
THE VEG PATCH

Applying a mulch to the veg patch simply means using a material to cover the top layer of soil. This may be done for a number of reasons with both organic (natural) and inorganic (man-made) 'mulches'.

Organic mulches include manure, leafmould, compost, grass mowings, or spent soil from pots and containers. They all encourage soil life, especially earthworms. These humble creatures are an absolutely essential component of healthy soil, playing a crucial role incorporating and cycling matter, as well as helping drainage via their extensive and labyrinthine tunnels. An organic mulch may be used to keep the soil warm in winter but cool in summer, prevent weeds from germinating by robbing them of the light, or conserve moisture if flopped down around a growing crop following a good soaking.

Newspaper and cardboard are considered as organic because they will rot down readily. They're especially useful when laid down underneath one of the mulches already mentioned, as a protective winter blanket.

Living mulches comprise growing a green manure to cover bare soil in gaps between cropping, or to protect the growing medium over winter from the erosive powers of wind and rain (not to be underestimated), especially on a slope. Legumes (the pea and bean family) such as clovers, lucerne (alfalfa) and field beans do a great job. They also fix atmospheric nitrogen in root nodules which is usefully exploited by the next batch of veggies grown on that piece. These, and others such as *Phacelia*, also add a goodly supply of organic matter to soils when they are cut down and turned-in before sowing.

Non-organic mulches include black plastic sheeting which is often left in place for a year or more to kill persistent weeds such as couch-grass or dock by totally preventing light penetration. Land can be still be worked with this sheeting in place by planting seedlings (or potato tubers) through carefully cut slits. Old carpet is another favourite amongst gardeners, used as a light-excluding mulch to suppress weeds and create bare soil without strenuous digging.

LOOKING AFTER PURPLE SPROUTING AND FROGS

Tidying purple sprouting broccoli

Purple sprouting broccoli might benefit from a little tending this week. Have a good rummage around the bottom of them. Clear away dead and yellowing leaves to the compost heap. Remove weeds at the same time. After this spruce-up they should look magnificent and handsome; fine plants with large leaves, a good crown and strong, thick stems.

Feeding...

Purple sprouting is a hungry brassica that likes to be bedded down in firm soil. To this end, tread the earth down around the base of each one with your heel and apply a thick mulch of well-rotted horse manure to the same area (keep a bucket and shovel in your vehicle for collecting manure from droppings on the road, then you'll always have a sack or two handy for this sort of job).

... staking

Lastly, stake each plant. A stout cane and baling twine are ideal for this purpose. Purple sprouting wants to grow quite large, 120 cm or more, and is susceptible to wind damage during gales. Good supports will hopefully prevent them from being rocked and having their roots loosened. Pigeon scarers in good working order are also vital. Made from compost bags cut into tassels and tied to tall canes,

NATURAL HISTORY IN THE GARDEN
Spindle Berries

Great pleasure may be had spotting spindle bushes in October. They're full of colour at this time of the year, sporting dark red leaves and a stack of bright pink, four-lobed berries. When ripe these split open to reveal four orange seeds.

Spindle was ruthlessly cut out of the countryside by farmers in the years after World War 2 on account of the fact that the black bean aphid, so commonly seen on broad beans in the early summer, loves to hang out on Spindle as an alternative host plant. A native to our shores, it is less out of favour these days, its wildlife and ornamental value being appreciated in these more environmentally enlightened times.

Spindle wood is tough and hard. The plant's name is a reminder of the common use it was put to in olden times, when weaving was an important job.

October, 2nd Week

they move and rustle in the breeze. There is little else to do now, except watch, wait and look forward to spring greens.

Frog conservation

Unashamedly, I love 'my' frogs. They're second to none when it comes to pest control, feasting on all sorts of garden nuisances. Their soft croaking from the ponds on a warm evening is a natural, beautiful music. Whilst clearing away spent courgette plants, I disturbed one of my friends; he hopped away to behind the greenhouse where there is plenty of scope for hiding, safe from neighbourhood cats. Make sure that your veg patch is frog-friendly by having lots of undisturbed places. Small piles of logs or stones that won't be moved, positioned strategically, ensure that the frogs are able to forage all areas of the plot with a safe hidey-hole always close by.

VEGETABLE SNIPPETS
SOME FACTS ABOUT BROCCOLI

A member of the 'cabbage tribe', purple sprouting broccoli heralds from Italy. The Romans adored this delectable vegetable. It was consumed in large quantities and with enthusiastic gusto at their infamously lavish and decadent banquets. By the early 1700s broccoli had been introduced to the UK but at this time it was very much an unfamiliar novelty at mealtime.

There are many different varieties and strains of broccoli. The familiar purple sprouting described here is a long-standing plant, being sown in the spring but not harvested until nearly a full year later. Calabrese is a quicker growing summer-cropping variety (from a spring sowing also). White sprouting is often confused with cauliflower.

All broccoli becomes tough if not cut and consumed when young. This is due to natural maturing processes within the plant, with internal sugars developing into fibre. Once this has occurred it is lost to the table as no amount of cooking and boiling will remedy the toughness.

The name broccoli comes from the Latin word 'brachium', which means 'strong arm'. This is a reference to the sturdy, branching nature of this popular garden food plant.

AUTUMN-SOWN BROAD BEANS AND SUNDAY FEASTS!

Why plant broad beans now?

Plant broad beans this week. Broads sown now come to fruition before a March planting. There are two big advantages to this. Firstly, the more advanced autumn sowing is rarely attacked in late spring by broad bean Enemy Number One, the blackfly, because it has passed the vulnerable stage when these pests are on the loose. Secondly, the broad bean season is advanced by two or three weeks.

Suitable variety

Several varieties of broad will over-winter quite happily, but 'Aquadulce' is a particularly reliable and early cropper. If the winter turns very cold then they will appreciate protection via a horticultural fleece. Keep your fingers crossed for a delicious and nutritious meal of autumn-sown broads before the end of May!

Preparing and planting

Prepare the plot firstly by weeding thoroughly, then digging in some fresh compost and raking level. At this time of year the soil is often quite damp so lay down wooden planks adjacent to where you want to mark the rows and work from these. The planks spread your bodyweight, minimising soil compaction, trampling and mess. Mark out the rows with canes and string, allowing 20 cm of space between. Simply press the thumbnail-sized beans into the fluffy soil to a depth of 7 cm. This is slightly deeper than for spring-sown broads, but the extra snugness helps them to endure the worst of the winter weather. Beans should be planted at 15 cm intervals. All being well, they should make a few inches of sturdy growth between now and New Year, then sit tight and wait for the spring rush.

Preparing a Sunday feast!

Usually I have to loosen my

NATURAL HISTORY IN THE GARDEN
Hibernating Small Tortoiseshell Butterflies

A few species of butterfly over-winter as adults. The small tortoiseshell commonly enters houses and sheds around now and settles with its wings folded together in a cool, quiet corner for the purpose of sleeping away the next few months. In this position the undersides of their wings disguise them as withered brown leaves. In the garden loose bark and the ivy-clad limbs of trees provide natural hibernation habitat for butterflies. Small tortoiseshells may over-winter communally.

Other hibernating species include the pale yellow brimstone and ragged-winged comma.

October, 3rd Week

trousers at the end of the week. Sunday is feast day for the family with many winter favourites now on the menu. A lot of work in the veg garden in the coming months will simply involve harvesting what is to be eaten on the day.

Lifting parsnips and other root veg for roasting cannot be hurried. Extracting a 60 cm long scorzonera thong in one piece is a challenge, and an achievement, in itself.

Swedes demand to be admired and their heady scent inhaled deeply before being washed, trimmed, peeled and cooked into a mash with spuds from store.

Leeks are in season from now until the end of March. Different varieties are cultivated to mature throughout both autumn and winter. Digging leeks for same-day consumption is a thrill in any weather. Fresh from the ground, they exude the most wonderful aroma. For me, just being outside whilst trimming the roots and 'flag' from a leek as dusk approaches is about as good as it gets (second only, perhaps, to eating the bounty).

VEGETABLE SNIPPETS

MEALTIME MAGIC

There is little which can compare with the pleasure to be had from sallying forth into kitchen-garden or down the allotment on a Sunday morning at this time of the year, and spending a good hour or so gathering the ingredients for a big meal. In the company of distant, peeling church bells and a quiet stillness which lends a timeless magic to the season of plenty, this is 'pottering' at its very best. Veggies fresh from the ground demand time to prepare, in the harvesting, rubbing, scrubbing and washing. This is an integral part of the fun. After admiring and considering what is to be eaten, bad bits must be removed and the produce readied for cooking. It cannot be rushed, in the same way that cultivating a tempting row of, say, swedes, is not a venture to be entered into in a hurry.

I'm a busy man and always have been. 'Burning the candle at both ends', my mother used to say some years ago. But growing your own veg tempers this. It reigns the home producer in to the natural rhythmic cycles of the seasons, working with forces which are so beautifully honed that careful planning and a little respectful fore-thought can reap plentiful rewards year-round. Sharing the bounty at mealtime, either with the children, with friends, or both, is a family ritual which has provided our household with some of its finest moments. There is nothing like a healthy hunger for good food to bring folk together.

ESSENTIAL GREENHOUSE WORK AND POTTING-ON PURSLANE

Pests and diseases in the greenhouse

Cleaning and disinfecting the greenhouse is not a job that I imagine anyone particularly looks forward to but, in the interests of continuing good crops, it has to be done. Diseases such as grey mould, or 'botrytis', thrive in the warm, enclosed conditions of the greenhouse environment. Their spores spread invisibly. These, and numerous other nasties, need to be cleansed in order to avoid future problems.

Clearing the inside

First thing is to remove the entire contents. Stack all your kit on wooden pallets ready for sorting and washing later. By this time of year there are always lots of spiders that have taken up residence in the greenhouse. Attempt to catch and release every one before disinfecting begins. Most spiders will drop down on a silken thread from their corner when stroked with a fine brush, and can be caught in a container held below. It's a time consuming and fiddly task but one that we undertake out of respect for these amazing hard-working little creatures.

Disinfecting

Then it's a case of mopping-out and washing-down the whole greenhouse interior with a biodegradable disinfectant, diluted to the manufacturer's recommended ratio. Washing the contents is next. Using plastic pots and trays makes cleaning easier. My staging, which can be

NATURAL HISTORY IN THE GARDEN
Hogweed

In areas of the plot left to go a bit wild, hogweed grows in abundance. It's a much maligned species and the sap can irritate the skin if the sun shines on it when still wet. None-the-less, it's a vital source of sustenance for declining bumble bees.

Having been in flower since June, displaying sturdy umbels of white flowers, this most common species of the parsley family will be setting seed at the moment. The skeletal, saucer-sized platters hold clusters of disc-shaped seeds smaller than an old half-penny. Heads held aloft on thick, browning stems, their ripe seeds scatter to the ground when disturbed by strong, gusting winds or are knocked by either gardener or foraging badgers.

October, 4th Week

built up and taken down as required, is plastic too. Disinfecting this is straightforward, using a large bucket of weak disinfectant to dunk everything into, with a toilet brush to dislodge caked-on potting compost and dirt.

Pot washing

It's an outside job and can be done little by little as and when equipment is needed for use. With a howling wind all around, leaves doing the manic dance of the autumn fall and temperatures low, it can feel thankless and tiresome. But when gales subside and warm late-season rays catch my cheeks and warm the shoulders, I'm in my heavenly element. Sitting on a stool, sleeves rolled up, sloshing and scrubbing mucky old pots which have raised all manner of veggies over the last few months, is an honest and wholesome task.

Winter purslane

The winter purslane, which was sown indoors during mid-September, should now be large enough for potting-on. Prepare 10 cm pots by filling with compost and pushing a hole in the middle about 5 cm deep to accommodate the roots. Loosen the seed tray soil by gently tearing out a clump of seedlings, taking utmost care not to damage roots or stalks. Gently hold the long oval leaves and patiently tease the seedling purslane plants apart. Select the biggest and strongest for potting-on.

Lower straggly roots into the prepared pots. Lovingly press the compost down to snuggle them in. They're then ready to go into the newly cleaned greenhouse. Kept moist, they should be growing enough fleshy round leaves to commence harvesting in a few weeks.

PLANTING GARLIC

November, 1st Week

Preparation

Now is the perfect time to plant garlic for over-wintering. It is a tough member of the onion tribe and a fairly reliable cropper as long as the ground is not too heavy. Planting garlic is a pretty straightforward task. As with most veg the preparation beforehand is all important. Clean the bed completely of weeds and give it a thorough dusting with dry wood ash if you've any to hand. No worries if not. Dig it in then rake to a fine and fluffy tilth. The bed is now ready.

Garlic can be planted at this time of year or in early spring. Be careful about choosing the right variety for the right time of year. You might be wise to select Messidrome or the purple-tinged Germidour for a late autumn sowing, varieties that are bursting to sprout soon if they have not already begun to do so. Other types such as Printador, that don't show green shoots until March or April, should be planted in the early spring.

Planting

Prize bulbs apart gently then separate individual cloves. Each will hopefully grow into a complete bulb for harvesting next June or July. Place them on top of the soil in blocks rather than lines, with 13 cm between each one. When they are in position firmly plunge them, one at a time, into the earth, pointed end uppermost, to a depth of 6 cm and smooth over. A cold

NATURAL HISTORY IN THE GARDEN
Wall Pellitory

Wall pellitory is a common plant in the West Country, jutting out from walls and cracks in stonework. It thrives wherever construction work by humans provides a suitable niche away from its favoured natural cliff and rocky outcrop habitats.

In November wall pellitory is a tufty, straggly plant, with elongated diamond-shaped green leaves borne on reddish stems. In mild weather it may still be flowering, displaying tiny pink blooms in clusters at the junction of leaf and stem. A cousin of the stinging nettle, it is an alternative food source for some of our aristocratic summer butterflies.

VEGETABLE SNIPPETS

SOME FACTS ABOUT
GARLIC

spell immediately after planting is hoped for as this stimulates the garlic into dividing and developing strong roots. Shoots should be showing well by New Year. All that is required is to keep weed free.

Garlic is a powerful little plant, consumed with great gusto in our household. Breaking up and planting four or five bulbs now, and again in the spring, is more than enough to give my family of four a home-grown garlic aroma all year round.

Originating in the Middle East, garlic as we know it is descended from wild stock and was developed by selective breeding way, way back long ago. It has been grown in Britain since before 1548 and is used in cooking as a flavour enhancer. Garlic (*Allium sativum*) is a particularly good foil for onions, tomatoes and ginger.

Endowed with a long and celebrated history in both culinary and medical fields, garlic is considered by many to be a 'natural tonic' on account of the many health promoting virtues with which it is credited.

The potent 'garlic aroma' associated with its consumption occurs when any of the plant cells are damaged. Violation via chopping, crushing or chewing prompts enzymes within the cells into a reaction. This is where the distinctive smell comes from. It's possible that this naturally occurring phenomenon evolved in garlic to counter grazing by herbivorous (plant-eating) animals.

Traditionally, complete bulbs (or heads) of garlic were hung up around doorways and chimney-breasts in the home to ward off evil spirits. Similarly, to keep vampires at bay, a clove or two was kept in a pocket about one's person.

WINTER WORK AND HARVESTING JERUSALEMS

Winter work

General tidy-up jobs are on the agenda in the edible garden this week. Removing dead leaves from crops, clearing patches of weeds that are beginning to try their luck and sorting out piles of canes, are all important jobs to do. You'll be removing places for slugs, snails and other pests to lurk, plus allowing easy access to the soil for robins and blackbirds. These birds are ever-watchful for pests that do venture out.

Working out next year's crop plan begins now. I reckon that it's easier to visualise what wants to go where when the plot is clearly defined. To this end, get busy clearing the edges. The pot marigolds, grown to suppress invasive couch-grass, are all but finished now. Pull spent plants up and chuck them onto the compost heap. Burn the rest of the weeds along the edge because there are always a few rogue lengths of couch, and lots of splinters of horsetail, in amongst them. Their presence can ruin a good compost heap.

Whilst cleaning the edge, throw soil inwards to create a shallow trench. Apart from being pleasing to look at, it will mark where the pot marigolds will be sown next spring (from seed saved this summer).

Jerusalem artichokes

Jerusalem artichokes come into season at this time of year. Cut your plants down to about 15 cm now. The top growth is thick and woody so reduce it to short lengths before it goes on the compost.

Underground, large knots of gnarled and twisted tubers have formed. They demand to be dug up with care, as even a tiny piece of tuber will grow again if left in the soil. One plant is harvested at a time, and the crop stored in a box of compost until needed.

Anything a potato can

NATURAL HISTORY IN THE GARDEN
Badgers in November

Badgers are less active this month. There are fewer feeding opportunities, especially if frosty weather sets in. They slow down their foraging and social activity in order to conserve vital energy and fat stores during the bleak weeks ahead.

November, 2nd Week

do, a Jerusalem can do too. However, it might be prudent not to eat huge amounts at any one sitting. Although they have a delectable, distinctive and unusual creamy taste and texture, over indulgence can cause tummy troubles for some people.

VEGETABLE SNIPPETS

FARTICHOKES!

Jerusalems contain a carbohydrate called inulin. Unlike other types of starch, such as those found in spuds for instance, 'inulin' is not absorbed by the body, and thus not utilised as an energy. A few folk have a slight intolerance to it and because of this, inulin can start to ferment inside the guts. Hence the tendency in some to suffer flatulence after partaking in the consumption of said veg. It's this quality that makes Jerusalems legendary around our dinner table, especially with the children. Due to these wind-breaking properties it is dubbed fartichoke, much to the amusement of the giggling kids, but not my frowning wife.

SUNFLOWERS, TEASELS AND FINCHES

As the cold weather really sets in there is great pleasure to be had in watching the birds that visit the plot for a feed. As well as providing nuts and other tidbits for our feathered friends, wildlife-friendly gardeners always cultivate certain plants especially for the birds.

Sunflowers

Sunflowers are good to grow. At this time of year thick stalks of the Giant Single variety still stand 3 metres or more. Their large heads, which at the peak of the season were incredible gold and brown glories the size of a dinner plate, now droop, dark and pecked ragged. They're high up on the menu for many seed eaters, including greenfinches. Leave sunflowers standing right through the winter, unless adverse weather snaps them first.

To please the eye during summer and feed the birds through winter, I sow sunflowers singly in pots of moist compost during March. Pop the black and white striped seeds in to a depth of 1.5 cm. They're strong growers in the greenhouse or on the window sill and should be big enough to plant out in early May. Allowing 60 cm or more at this stage may seem a bit extravagant but be generous with your sunflowers when it comes to giving them space (and water during dry spells). Your charges will respond to a fortnightly dose of nettle and comfrey feed with energetic growth and spectacular flowers from high summer onwards.

Teasels

Another provider of nourishment for birds in winter is the teasel. By November specimens become a crisp brown skeleton, 2 metres tall, with numerous stems supporting

NATURAL HISTORY IN THE GARDEN
'Jenny' Wren

Look out for the diminutive wren this month. With woody plants now all but bare, these stumpy little birds can be spotted as they flit between trees and bushes around the garden. Wrens are less than 10 cm in length and sport chestnut-brown upper parts with lighter colouration below. A bandit-like eye stripe is distinctive, and so too the short, cocked tail. They are active, like clockwork toys, constantly bobbing up and down as they tick-tack along branches in search of insect food. Wrens have a powerful song and at this time of year listen out for their short, sharp, 'tit-tit-tit' delivery. It is slightly harsher than the not dissimilar robin.

November, 3rd Week

dozens of spiky, egg-shaped seed heads. It is a magnet for goldfinches. These birds have beaks which are perfectly evolved to fit into the depths of these 'hedgehogs' and extract the seeds. A flock of goldfinches is known as a 'charm', and when travelling thus they have a beautiful call which sounds like a thick and precious dripping liquid.

My veg patch has teasels popping up all over the place, descendants of those that were introduced from a packet of mixed wildflower seeds. They develop a low rosette of leaves, studded with soft spikes, and are easy to identify. I'll move these self-sown plants to a more appropriate growing site any time from October to March. Borne on the 'hedgehog' in high summer, purple teasel flowers are very attractive to many long-tongued insects.

VEGETABLE SNIPPETS

FULLER'S TEASEL

Both the common teasel and fuller's teasel are valuable additions to the rough corners of a vegetable patch, or integrated into the flower border. Their wildlife value in terms of attracting pollinating insects is excellent. Subsequently the seeds are attractive to birds. The plants themselves are physically impressive. They lend an air of majestic structure to a garden, especially if allowed to stand throughout the winter when they can become beautifully decorated with frost.

Teasels are easy to grow in all soils (including heavy clay) as long as their position is a sunny one. They self-seed freely, and in subsequent years will need to be kept in check with regular weeding sessions to remove the flat rosettes of tough green leaves sported by immature seedlings. This is not too demanding because as first-year youngsters they send down a creamy central tap-root which is lifted easily enough when loosened with the aid of a border fork.

Fuller's teasel differs from the common variety in that the seeded flower head develops hooked barbs as opposed to spikes which are straight. This quality was exploited initially during the agricultural depression from 1650 to 1750 in areas such as North Somerset, where fuller's teasel became an important crop. The dried seedheads were employed in the woollen industry for raising the nap on manufactured cloth.

Fuller's teasel has its reputed medicinal uses too. Ointments made from the roots were used to treat warts. An infusion of dried root was believed to be beneficial to one's stomach, to enhance one's appetite and clean the liver.

IN THE VEG STORE AND PUTTING GLOBE ARTICHOKES TO BED

A cold and wet weekend is an ideal time to get into the vegetable store. Veggies kept under cover in a frost-free place require regular inspections. Anything going rotten or 'on the turn' must be either discarded to the compost (except potatoes, which should be binned) or used immediately. Keep a keen eye on your stash of stored winter veg via thorough fortnightly check-ups. Handle everything, turning and pressing gently.

The onion tribe
Garlic and shallots are fairly reliable storers, although uneaten winter garlic varieties could be starting to sprout. A handful of shallots may go soft and need removing from storage trays. Red onions are much poorer storers than maincrops and should be on the menu regularly until supplies are gone. They are wonderful roasted, caramelised or raw, and their seasonality simply amplifies their deliciousness.

Some maincrop onions get chucked at each checking. Get rid of any gone soft or showing green shoots and be ever-watchful around their roots. The odd one rots from here, oozing a reddish-brown slime that hollows out the middle. Early detection is vital as the dripping goo may contaminate other onions and smells appalling. These losses are inevitable. It is always sad to condemn any food crops, especially after

NATURAL HISTORY IN THE GARDEN
Redwings and Fieldfares

Over-wintering thrushes are in the country around now. Redwings and fieldfares breed in Northern Europe and Scandinavia but journey to our warmer climes out of season, where the living is not so harsh.

Redwings are brown on top with a red sash along their flank and under the wing. At 25 cm, fieldfares are nearly 5 cm larger than their cousins.

They display slate-grey heads and rumps with a rusty brown back and dark tail. Both species show classic thrush-mottled breasts. They like to feed communally, scrounging around the country larder for hawthorn berries and windfall apples. Redwing flocks may be heard at night-time passing overhead, keeping in close contact via plaintive, hissing calls.

November, 4th Week

lovingly tending them through the summer and making every effort to provide the best storage conditions. But take heart nevertheless, as every rotten onion removed prolongs the keeping quality of the others. If you can, cultivate enough to withstand these losses.

Potatoes

Potatoes demand to be smelled as well as handled. Those in sacks can suffer heavy losses if just one spud rots and it spreads. A deep inhalation, head down in the sack, is recommended. I know from experience that I'll sniff out a rotten spud if there is one, because the unforgettable smell is truly ghastly. In spite of meticulous preparation, washing and drying, avoiding heavy losses is all part of the fun! If the veg store develops any unusual aroma, check the tatties first. Those stored one-deep in plastic fruit trays are far easier to monitor but must be kept in the dark. Coats draped over the tray stack is a good option.

Squashes

Squashes store differently according to variety. I've always struggled to stop my Butternuts from going mouldy much beyond this time of year. If a failing Butternut is caught early, most of it can be saved if eaten at once. It's a fantastic ingredient for winter-warmer soups. Acorn and Spaghetti squashes, plus other thick-skinned orangey and bluish 'onion' types store for far longer. With luck they could be fine well into New Year and saved until the other varieties have been eaten.

Winter care for globe artichokes

Outside, globe artichokes don't relish severe weather. With this in mind, now's the time to put them to bed for the winter. Cut down fresh growth to about 20 cm and apply a thick mulch of leaves around the base of the plant, but not over the crown. Criss-cross twigs and sticks on top of this, then one or two layers of horticultural fleece which is pegged down and held with heavier planks of wood. This should keep the globes nice and cosy even in extreme conditions, but still allow air to circulate and prevent the crown from rotting.

This job is often undertaken in biting cold and persistent heavy rain, in stark contrast to the beautiful, hot conditions of mid-summer, when the heads are fat and ready for cutting. These extremes really are the 'spice of life' for those of us who love being out in the weather whatever it's up to.

WINTER DIGGING

November, 5th Week

Why bother?

If you garden on heavy soil then start to dig over your vegetable plot this week. The aim is to turn over every vacant piece of ground during the next two or three months. If much of it is covered by a green manure crop then take the hoe to it. Cut it down before digging in. The goodness in the plants is released into the soil as they decompose. Elsewhere, leafmould and compost mulches that were applied in the autumn can be turned in too.

Although there are many schools of thought on the merits of digging in relation to growing vegetables, I personally favour this regime for many reasons. They all ultimately lead to the production of wholesome, delicious food.

Digging the soil to a depth of one spit (the length of a spade head) exposes it to the winter elements. A freshly dug piece of ground looks like a still-life of choppy waters at sea. By springtime, this will have been weathered by the forces of rain, wind and frost, into a calmer, smoother picture. The resulting friable soil is easily turned into a seedbed when spring sowing time comes around again.

Robins

The rush of spring work will be much easier to manage if you've prepared the ground well in advance. Relish also the closeness of your relationship with the earth whilst toiling. Winter digging is part of this ongoing partnership. Adopt a tender, loving and careful approach year on year. Work with the soil and continually renew your acquaintance with it. Friendly robins are almost constant companions at this time. They drop in fearlessly, hopping from clod to clod, stopping, tilting their heads to one side listening, then diving into a crack or hollow to snaffle a tasty morsel. Robins find rich pickings where the ground is disturbed and account for many soil pests at the same time. Digging when in the company of these beady-eyed little birds is great fun. They give us gardeners an excuse to take regular pauses, straighten our backs and survey the work in progress.

Keeping it easy

Digging is a strenuous activity. It's easy to get lost in the rhythmic meditation of the job, which can lead to back-ache the next day. Don't dig for more than half an hour before taking a break and doing something else. Undertake each turn of sod slowly, methodically and with respect. This is a labour of

VEGETABLE SNIPPETS
SOIL ORGANIC MATTER (SOM)

love. Keep your back as straight as possible. Let knees, thighs and arms take the strain.

Working on wet ground is extra hard work and can do more harm than good by compressing the soil structure. If great clods are sticking to your boots, then it's too wet to dig. Where ground is sloping, erosion and physical effort can be minimised by working along the contour facing uphill. With a sensible and realistic approach to digging this annual task may be tackled manually for many years to come.

Soil Organic Matter (SOM) is any part of the soil that once lived. From both plants and animals, it is dead stuff in varying degrees of decomposition. SOM is highly nutritious and therefore an essential ingredient in the production of home-grown veggies. It is, however, only a small component of most garden soils in this country, comprising just 2% to 5% of the good earth that most of us have to play with.

When fully rotted, SOM is called 'humus'. It's dark brown, allows easy passage of water (is porous), spongy to touch and has a rich smell. It is in this state when most of its nutrients are available to crops.

Another key element of SOM is the part it plays in a healthy structure. By opening up the land, it introduces plenty of oxygen. It provides a great habitat and high sources of energy for creatures living in this domain, from earthworms to microbes. These all have a crucial role to play in the well-being of your veg plot.

It is also fantastic for conditioning soils. When heavy and/or compacted and difficult to work, SOM makes the soil more friable and much easier going. Where the growing medium is too light and/or free-draining, SOM binds particles together which gives the soil bulk and body.

SOM does, however, have its limitations. Garden compost can harbour plant viruses and / or diseases if infected material has been added to the refuse heap instead of being burnt. Similarly, perennial weed seeds can survive humification and frequently germinate when compost is applied to the plot.

Farmyard manure must be well-rotted lest it give off ammonia, while fresh straw and leaves can rob the soil of nitrogen as they rot down, which can cause a nutrient imbalance. They should be partially decomposed at the very least when incorporated into the ground.

TENDING WINTER ONIONS

December, 1st Week

Get busy this week in the winter onion bed. Radar onions, which were planted as sets in September, should have taken well. Healthy greenery on top indicates strong rooting down below, which is vital for a heavy crop. At this time of year, the onions have settled down and won't make any visible growth for a while. Now is a perfect opportunity to get in amongst them and have a good tidy up.

Weeding

Even young weeds have tenacious roots. They need to be teased out whole. A kitchen fork is ideal for gently extracting them from the damp soil. Don't be afraid to drop onto your hands and knees for this one! Work slowly forwards along the row, filling a bucket with young weeds as you go. The bed soon cleans up and onions will show off handsomely in their lines. When this job is done, employ a hoe. Exercise it carefully, moving backwards, pushing and pulling the blade back and fore. Rough up the soil surface and disturb any tiny weeds that are just germinating. I thoroughly enjoy this job, not least because it feels so satisfying to be genuinely weeding and hoeing in December.

Feeding

All members of the onion family appreciate the goodness contained in wood ash. Radar is no exception. Sprinkle down and hoe in a top dressing of wood ash during early spring. To this end, save and store all ash from home fires and bonfires. It needs to be kept dry prior to use.

NATURAL HISTORY IN THE GARDEN
Badgers in December

Female (sow) badgers may have held fertilised eggs in their bodies since last spring, but now is the time when amazing internal processes cause the egg to become implanted in the womb. Litters usually comprise two or three cubs, to be born any time from mid-January to the end of March.

VEGETABLE SNIPPETS

WOOD ASH

Wood ash is a useful by-product of bonfires in the garden. Having a regular burn-up is an important job. Fires cleanly and effectively get rid of diseased plant material and deal with troublesome weeds such as thick-rooted dandelions, persistent creeping buttercup, and the seemingly impossible-to-kill trio of bindweed, couch grass and horsetail. It's a lovely thing to do, standing beside a crackling blaze, warming your hands, absorbing the deliciously romantic aroma of wood smoke into clothes and hair.

Fire is a magical, elemental force. Although not quite living it is non-the-less very much alive. In no time fire transforms harmful waste into a valuable resource which will do the veggies no end of good.

Wood ash is almost pure potash. This is beneficial to all crops in varying degrees. Sugary and starchy veg demand it to help their metabolism. For instance, spuds love it when sprinkled between the rows as a 'top dressing' prior to earthing them up in the summer. Potash is high in potassium which is a nutrient that encourages flowering and fruiting. Hence it's good for beans, curcubits (squashes, marrows, cucumbers and the like), tomatoes and others that set a fruiting crop. Shake a handful around the base of these plants when they're coming to this stage of their lives.

A week or so before sowing seeds, apply wood ash to a prepared seedbed at the rate of about one heaped trowel per square metre. It'll be appreciated by the developing tiddlers.

101

WASPS, LEAFMOULD AND BRASSICAS

Wasps and leafmould

Throughout the summer months, one of my leafmould bins was squatted in by wasps. To begin with, their hectic activity was a bit of a worry. However, we lived happily in the same shared space. I took care to always work slowly, quietly and deliberately, so as not to disturb the nest when in close proximity. Much time was spent watching the wasps in their daytime toil, lifting out from and dropping into a small hole at the back of the leaf pile.

This relationship was mutually beneficial. In return for being left in peace, the colony of up to 2000 wasps accounted for countless insect pests including aphids and caterpillars, which they need to feed their larvae. In fact the wasps kept a dozen purple sprouting plants, growing immediately adjacent to the nest, completely free of cabbage white caterpillars all summer long.

The cold weather of winter eventually killed off the drone and worker wasps. Hopefully the fertilised queen crept away to somewhere safe for hibernation. What they left was access to fifteen month old leafmould, beautifully decomposed to a soft, crumbly texture. Rather than spread this onto the veg plot for digging in, I've decided to use it as the finest quality potting compost. To this end, the growing medium has been shovelled into old plastic compost bags, and transferred to the greenhouse ready for use. Well rotted leafmould is

NATURAL HISTORY IN THE GARDEN
Blue Tits

Look out for Blue tits. These 12 cm long, lively little blue and yellow customers with white faces are a familiar sight amongst the trees and shrubby areas in most gardens. During wintertime they often flock together with other species such as chaffinches, nuthatches, Great and Coal tits. A meagre ration is eked out communally. Blue tits hunt amongst tree branches, searching for insects and spiders in nooks, crannies and under loose bark. They often dangle acrobatically upside-down in order to get at a tasty morsel.

December, 2nd Week

perfect for sowing seeds into. For potting-on seedlings, I'll mix the leafmould with molehill soil to a ratio of 50/50.

Brassicas

All brassicas, including purple sprouting broccoli, should have attention lavished on them this week. Tread down the soil around the base of their stems and re-fasten supporting canes. Yellowing bottom leaves must constantly be picked off and cleared away to keep the plants as clean and healthy as possible. All the cabbage family are gross feeders. Flop a thick mulch of well-rotted manure around their firmed-in stem bases.

VEGETABLE SNIPPETS

A BRIEF HISTORY OF ALLOTMENTS

The history of allotments dates back to at least 1066, and the Feudal system established by William the Conqueror. In those days, ruling gentry lorded it over their serfs who were allowed to cultivate strips of land in the open Manorial fields. Enclosure of these in the 1500s removed some of these rights. A hundred-odd years later, slave-driven workers had been re-classified as peasants. As part of their meagre ration, they were permitted to grow foodstuffs next to their tied cottages (known as 'pottagers').

The next wave of enclosure occurred between 1760 and 1818. Open and common land was grabbed on an enormous scale. During that time, five thousand Acts of Parliament secured seven million acres into private ownership. A further seventeen million acres were simply taken, principally by the landed gentry and yeoman farmers. Peasants were now the 'labouring poor'. Some Parish and private ground was rented out to those folk for veg production but opposition to the needs of the workers was rife. Consequently, land allotted for such purposes was few and far between. Where it did exist, strict rules applied. For instance, in some places gardening was prohibited on weekdays between 6am and 6pm, plus all day Sunday.

Laws were passed in 1845 to legally secure cheap and accessible allotments. Although motivation was arguably to keep the working classes out of the pub when not slogging away for someone else, this was a momentous change. Allotments of a practical size for purpose became established and popular, especially in urban areas. In 1919 and 1945, immediately following the two World Wars, well over a million allotments were actively in service.

Radical societal and land-use changes since then have seen much 'leisure garden' space lost to development schemes and disuse, but statutory regulations demand that authorities provide these areas for use by the Council Tax-paying public. Modern sites are havens for people of all races, ages, genders, political persuasions and classes: individuals who seek solace in the company of soil and what it can produce.

Enthusiasm for allotment gardening comes and goes like most fads and fashions. The first thing to do if the prospect takes your fancy is to visit the local Council offices, enquire, and (more than likely) put your name on a waiting list. Depending on the mood of the day, an opportunity to get deep down and dirty may come along sooner than you think. Be prepared!

SHALLOTS

December, 3rd Week

Plant your shallots this week. Prolific and reliable members of the onion tribe, they're traditionally planted on the shortest day of the year and harvested on the longest. Although the crop is not always ripe for lifting on June 21st, why not get your charges in the ground on mid-winters day? Select the best of last season's crop; those that are firm, whole and about 2.5 cm or so across, or purchase some from the garden centre.

Site selection and preparation

Shallots are sun-lovers, a fact to be considered when a growing site is chosen. Clean weeds from the plot meticulously prior to planting, then lightly fork the soil over. Apply a liberal dusting of dry wood ash and rake it in. Because shallots like to grow in firm ground, tread it down with small sideways steps all over. This is called doing the 'Gardener's Shuffle'. Give

the bed one more light raking before it receives the shiny brown bulbs.

Planting

Tie string between two canes to keep your planting lines straight. These will be easier to maintain and keep weed-free with a hoe than wonky rows. Next, carefully rub or cut off all loose, flaky outer skin and stalk before planting at 23 cm intervals in rows 30 cm apart. Make a little planting nest with

NATURAL HISTORY IN THE GARDEN
Foxes

From the silent depths of a long cold night, listen out for the unearthly screaming wails of foxes. This primeval noise is the female (vixen) calling out to potential mates in the vicinity. The mating season occurs from December until February. During this time the male (dog) foxes travel extensively over large areas of town and country looking for a suitable partner.

Once contact has been established the couple spend many days by each other's side. The dog will follow the vixen as if in a spell, and may be seen doing so even in broad daylight. After three weeks or so mating takes place many times. The foxes may become so embroiled in their business that they become locked together and oblivious to what is going on around them.

your thumb, and press each set in gently to half its depth. Then firm soil back around the set with thumb and first finger. Use both hands.

Aftercare

Shallots need to be inspected regularly for a couple of weeks after planting, until their roots have taken anchor. Cats, birds and frost can all lift them out of position, as can the growing roots if merely pushed into the ground and not nestled down securely. Firm any sets that are showing signs of looseness during your daily rounds.

All being well, they should be showing green shoots in a few weeks. Apart from the initial care and attention during rooting, shallots require only to be kept moist and weed-free in order to give a really big return for the space occupied.

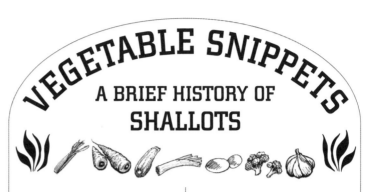

VEGETABLE SNIPPETS
A BRIEF HISTORY OF
SHALLOTS

Shallots are part of the onion family, which boasts 450 species worldwide. This veg was a staple foodstuff in ancient Egypt. Shallots were introduced to European palates as 'eschallots' in the 12th century by returning Crusaders. Their onion-like bounty heralded from the ancient Palestinian (Canaan) city of Ascalon, from where they were believed to have originated.

MULCHING WITH BRACKEN

December, 4th Week

The threat of harsh weather and frozen ground is ever-present at this time of year. Freezing conditions are both good and bad. Good, because the cold kills off a lot of soil-borne pests, and because the action of freeze/thaw leaves previously dug soil loose and friable in the spring. But frozen ground can also be a problem when it comes to lifting roots and other crops that are still standing on the plot. Try to minimise the risk of having much needed food crops locked in to frozen earth by applying a thick mulch. Straw or bracken is ideal for this purpose.

Harvesting

Bracken is freely available on areas of common land locally and it costs nothing to cut and gather apart from the time and effort. Use shears for cutting low down, then rake it into piles before stuffing it into plastic bags. Even damp and rotting bracken has a lot of sharp, woody splinters. These can slice the fingers painfully, similar to a paper-cut, so always wear gloves for this job.

Protecting roots and leeks

Once in amongst your veg, spread the bracken thickly over parsnips, salsify, scorzonera and Jerusalem artichokes. Lines of 'snips may have to be marked with canes, but the others should have enough tops to show their position amongst the cosy bedding.

NATURAL HISTORY IN THE GARDEN
Cotoneaster Berries

There are many different types of cotoneaster. They are red-berried trees or shrubs with glossy green leaves. The abundant crop they carry in the winter months is often left untouched until late in mild seasons, but could prove to be a lifesaver for blackbirds and other berry-eaters during prolonged cold weather.

This final month of the year is the perfect time for lingering in the garden. There's always something to stimulate the senses and lift the heart, be it massive, drifting cloudscapes, intricate patterns traced by bare-stemmed tree branches, the chattering machine-gun rattle of a handsome magpie, or any amount of Nature's other wonders.

Leeks are essential eating right now. To ensure access in even really hard weather, mulch around their bases and between rows.

Feeding the birds

These can be tough times for the birds which afford such wonderful year-round company in the garden. A few handfuls of mixed seeds, scattered along paths and away from cat danger, are always well appreciated by our feathered friends.

VEGETABLE SNIPPETS
BRACKEN USE
THROUGH HISTORY

Since Neolithic Times, some 3000 BC, bracken has been put to a multitude of uses by humans.

Dried bracken makes excellent litter for livestock. The Romans thought of it so highly that they used it as bedding for themselves as well as their animals. It has been commandeered as fuel for heating purposes and the baking and brewing processes. Bracken was widely employed in the construction of dwellings, especially for thatching. As compost in the gardens of large estate houses, well-rotted bracken was used as a bulky conditioning material which both lightened-up heavy soil and bulked-up light soils.

Latterly, in the 1800s, it was used for the production of potash. In this form, it was an integral part of early industrial processes including glass and soap making, as well as the manufacture of detergents. Throughout this time bracken continued to be widely burnt for domestic purposes also.

Nowadays quantities may be mechanically harvested, allowed to decompose, then be bagged up and sold in garden centres under various names including 'Forest Bark'.

Many authorities consider that there is now too much of this plant growing in the UK. One theory for the explosive spread of bracken in many areas is that, now it is seldom utilised and therefore cut less, rotting fronds act as a protective 'self-mulch' over the tender crowns in winter-time. Instead of getting nipped in the bud during freezing cold spells, it is surviving and thriving. As a resource for the gardener, it is widely available for the taking.

PLANNING FOR THE SEASON AHEAD

January, 1st Week

With the arrival of a new year, get busy planning your planting schedule for the coming season. If you've not already got most of the seeds in hand, place an order with a reputable and reliable company over the phone or internet, or pop down the garden centre for a browse (I prefer the latter).

Making a planting plan

I'm a meticulous note-taker, and at times like this my scribblings are invaluable for plotting out what to plant and when. Writing down a planting plan, month-by-month for the whole year, keeps tasks in proportion and under control. I'm clearly able to see how the veg garden will develop. As each month rolls along, I can sort out the seeds that will be handled for those four-odd weeks. This careful attention to detail gets me in the mood for what lies ahead and ensures that when the really manic seed-sowing months of March, April and May arrive, I'm not overwhelmed by jobs to do. Weather conditions will affect planting times. Wet or cold spells can force the postponement of sowing certain crops, especially those sown outside, direct into the soil. Flexibility is needed and an instinctive ability to seize the right moment for the right job.

Rotating crops

If possible, avoid growing the same crop on the same patch of ground twice in a row. Aim ideally at keeping a three-year gap. By rotating crops in this way, soil dwelling pests that take a particular fancy to any one type of veg are prevented from becoming established by moving their chosen food source elsewhere. Also, different veggies extract different nutrients and goodness from the earth. Continually changing the positions of crops prevents the soil from becoming unbalanced or

NATURAL HISTORY IN THE GARDEN
Robins

One of the most common birds to be heard in this part of winter is the red-breasted cock robin. He likes to sit high up in the branches of a tree and mark his territory with a song that is a thin, watery, sad but sweet warble.

nutritionally depleted. Don't get too hung up on this if your growing space is limited, though. Just remember that, as a rule, well-manured ground which grows brassicas this year will be good for roots (including potatoes) next, followed by peas, beans, onions, salads or fruiting veg the year after that. Once again, pen and paper are extremely helpful as one literally maps out a crop plan.

VEGETABLE SNIPPETS
SOIL
HAND TEXTURE TEST

Most UK soils are formed by the gradual breaking down (erosion) of underlying rocks (parent material) over geological time, which is measured over millions of years.

Soil textures are known as sandy, silty or clayey, depending on the dominant particle size from which it comprises (in descending order, sand is the largest, then silt, then clay). These classifications have important repercussions in the veg patch in terms of moisture and nutrient holding abilities. For example, a light sandy soil is free-draining, whereas heavy clays are not. A lighter soil is liable to become impoverished quicker than a heavy medium which can retain much of the essential goodness for longer. Those with a silty disposition are prone to erosion, especially when wet and on a slope.

Chalky soils occur over large areas of the UK. These tend to be thin and alkaline. Adding copious amounts of bulky farmyard manure and compost creates favourable conditions for fruit, the cabbage tribe plus peas and beans in particular.

Loamy soils, where there is a balanced mix of different sized particles, are ideal for veg cultivation. They warm up quickly in the spring, are comfortable to work and retain both water and nutrients well without becoming saturated.

Texture is easy to determine on the plot. Gather a golf-ball sized ball of soil and massage in your hands. Water can be added if needs be, so that it is uniformly moist but not wet. When the ball has been massaged to an even consistency it is ready to tell its tale.

By moulding it into balls, sausages and rings, the main texture groups can be determined as follows:

No ball = sand
Crumbly ball = loamy sand
Firm ball = sandy loam
Crumbly sausage = silt loam
Firm sausage = medium loam
Forms a ring = clay loam
Shiny ring = clay
Shiny gritty ring = sandy clay

PLANTING BUSH APPLES

January, 2nd Week

This is a good time of year to plant apple trees, as long as the weather is not too severe and the ground isn't waterlogged or frozen. There's enormous pleasure to be had from tending a collection of fruit trees.

Bush trees

'Bush' trees are ideal where space is limited. With apples, the final size of the tree is dictated by what 'rootstock' the variety is 'grafted' onto. Bush apples can be grown on a number of different rootstock, but at home we plump for what is called 'M26', which is relatively dwarfing. Full-grown trees should attain no more than roughly 3 metres in height, thus fruit will remains within easy reach for harvesting. Plant bush apples with 3.6 metre spacing.

Compatible varieties

Growing varieties of apple that come into blossom together is an important factor, as most apple trees will set a better crop if pollinated by another variety flowering at more or less the same time. Merton Knave, Worcester Permain, Sunset, Blenheim Orange, Pixie and Wagener are all dessert (or 'eating') apples. They should provide ripe fruit to munch on from late-August (Merton Knave, picked and eaten straight from the tree) through to March (Wagener, picked in October and stored carefully).

Purchasing

I purchase fruit trees as one-year old 'maiden whips', which means that they are a single stem (scion) grafted onto the rootstock. I'm also very fussy about where they come from. I only source trees from nurseries where staff can answer all queries with authority. Delivery to the door is crucial too, because often there is no time for big trips out.

Planting

The maidens should arrive tied in bags, with straw or similar wrapped around the roots. They can be kept under cover like this for a while if planting conditions are unfavourable at that time. A sunny site should have been thoroughly cleared and weeded beforehand. Plant the young apple trees with as little disturbance to the soil as possible. Lever a slot open with a spade and spread the roots down into this gently with your fingers. If the soil is fairly good there is no need for fertilisers. Fresh manure is definitely a no-no because it will burn the root tips.

Great care must be taken at this stage to ensure that the junction of scion and rootstock is kept well clear of the ground. Ensure the soil mark on the stem coincides with the soil level after the slot has been firmly but carefully closed snugly around the roots with lightly stamping feet. Air pockets must also be avoided or else the roots, and therefore the tree, are liable to suffer. No staking is needed for bush apples planted like this. Any natural movement of stem in the wind will only encourage strong root growth. All that remains, for now, is to apply a goodly bucket of water, one per tree, and to keep well moist throughout the first summer.

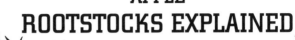

FRUIT SNIPPETS
APPLE
ROOTSTOCKS EXPLAINED

Rootstocks are prefixed with 'M' or 'MM'. The former were developed at the East Malling Research Station in Kent, while the latter came to fruition at Merton Malling. Between them, they have revolutionised apple cultivation for the home producer. Trees can be nurtured on rootstock which is adapted to suit local conditions and available space, from good soil to poor, large acreages to backyards and pots.

• M27 is 'extremely dwarfing'. Fully cropping after five years, an apple tree on this rootstock will never grow taller than an average man. Trees should be staked for support, and surrounding soil should be well fed.

• M9 is 'very dwarfing', with maximum cropping potential realised a year or two later than those on M27. 3 metres is the usual full-grown height. They will need full-time supports and seasonal feeding. M9 is a good choice for apple trees in a small garden.

• M26 is 'dwarfing', and what I cultivate my bush apples on.

• MM106 is deemed 'semi-dwarfing' or 'semi vigorous' and used to grow Half-Standard trees. They reach maximum cropping potential after 8 years, but will be producing fruits in half that time. Fully grown MM106 apple trees may be up to 6 metres in height, and are thus ideal for medium-sized gardens.

• MM111(M25) is the rootstock of choice if a vigorous Standard tree is desired. It's the perfect rootstock for large gardens or orchards. Within 10 years a heavy crop will bear annually, but take care whilst picking - a ladder will be essential for reaching the upper-most boughs and branches.

CUPS OF TEA AND COBNUTS

January, 3rd Week

Tea

This can be a frustrating time of year. It doesn't happen very often, but occasionally the hectic work/family agenda means that there's not a lot of time to get outside and tend the land, beyond having a quick cup of tea and a look. Happily, by doing a little and often, we can keep pretty well on top of everything and relax whilst there isn't much demanding immediate attention. Nevertheless, if you like getting your hands in the soil as much as possible weekends offer welcome respite from other commitments and refreshing opportunities to have a good scratch round while harvesting the week's veg. Don't worry if you're still trying to work out where to plant crops for this coming season and constantly changing your mind – so am I!

Cobnuts

Nothing stays still in the garden. Spring feels almost touchable on days when the wind drops and the sun shines. In the orchard I'm cultivating cobnuts and filberts, with four varieties on the go: Nottingham Cob (aka Pearsons Prolific), Cosford Cob, Lamberts Filbert (aka Kent Cob), and White Filbert. They're all domesticated varieties of the southern hazel, and sourced from a reliable nursery.

Catkins, which are the male flowers, festoon each bush. Some may be open already. They resemble lamb's tails and, in a breeze, little clouds of pollen are released and carried in the air. Female flowers, which are minute red stars borne at the tips of fat buds, receive this pollen and

NATURAL HISTORY IN THE GARDEN
Long-tailed Tits

Long-tailed tits are tiny black, grey and pink birds. In adults, over half of their 14 cm length is made up by their tails. Long-tailed tits always live in groups except during the breeding season and there are often little flocks of them to be seen, flitting and dancing through the leafless canopy of trees growing just beyond our back garden wall. They search for spiders and insects hiding in amongst the branches. Long-tailed tits are easily identified by their distinctive tail feathers and mischievous twittering calls.

VEGETABLE SNIPPETS

HERB TEAS AND CABBAGE WATER

fertilisation occurs. Keep your fingers crossed for a bumper crop of nuts this autumn.

Cobnuts and filberts can be planted at this time of year if bare-rooted, or any time if pot-grown. Either way, they should be cultivated with at least 90 cm all round. They prefer a deep, moist soil in sheltered areas and tolerate light shade. I've planted mine to create a food-producing hedge.

Herbs from the garden are perfect for making a cup of refreshing, stimulating tea. At this time of year choice may not be so great, but if any young sprigs are available they can be popped into a mug and boiling water applied, no fuss, no bother. Alternatively a selection of leaves, dried during summer, can be used. Fennel, lavender and mint are obvious candidates.

Truth is that I rarely, if ever, make tea out of herbs growing in the garden. In the hot beverage department, any traditional (organic) tea that is fair-traded is good by me, with a splash of this and a spoonful of that, for nursing and sipping whilst having a think and a look on a cold winter's day. Having said that, I am rather partial to a steaming hot mug of cabbage water, especially with a bit of vegetable stock stirred in to savoury it up a bit.

CHITTING POTATOES

Potatoes are a valuable and versatile vegetable. By cultivating different types of spud, you'll be able to keep the family well supplied with these tasty tubers for much of the year.

Potato types

First Early spuds offer 'new' potatoes fresh from the earth around mid-summer. Second Earlies are ready later in the season (July). Maincrop varieties will store well for use throughout the winter. Growing a Salad potato such as Pink Fir Apple is a good idea if ground is available. Cooked 'til tender, then tossed in an olive-oil based dressing or similar, they add another dimension to potato consumption.

Varieties

As well as different types of spud, there are also numerous varieties. Each possesses their own particular strengths and qualities. It's well worth taking the time to find out what varieties are suited to the locality where they are to be planted. I can't recommend Second Early Kestrel highly enough because they're reliable, taste wonderful and succeed in a wide range of containers and plots. Why not experiment with other varieties? Read any technical blurb to guide you, be bold and have a go!

Chitting

You'll likely not be planting spuds until March, weather permitting. However, work for this year's crop begins now. Purchase stock of certified disease-free seed potatoes this week. Get them in hand early in the year and set them out for

NATURAL HISTORY IN THE GARDEN
Badgers in January

Look out for shallow holes and scratched up soil in and around the garden. These are 'snuffle holes' and are the work of badgers. These handsome black and white fellows, who have made a gentle living in our countryside for thousands of years, are pretty quiet and inactive at this time of year. However a mild spell will tempt them out of their underground home, or sett, to look for earthworms, their favourite food, and beetles.

VEGETABLE SNIPPETS

TO CHIT OR NOT TO CHIT

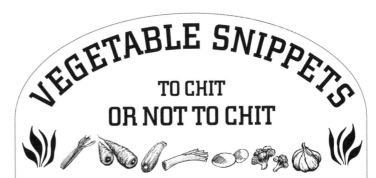

'chitting'. Each spud has a number of 'eyes' which are barely discernable now, but will soon produce shoots. These shoots, which should be dark and stout, are the 'chits'.

To chit your spuds just set them out in trays in a single layer, with eyes uppermost. Touching is fine. Egg-boxes are perfect. Keep them in a cool, light and frost-free place; the greenhouse is ideal. If severe weather threatens, cover your spuds with newspaper to protect them from any risk of frost. No water is needed, just a check-over from time to time. If the shoots appear spindly and/or pale in colour, then more daylight is required. Spuds demand careful handling at all times, as they bruise easily. Chitting potatoes always gives me a little thrill because it heralds the beginning of the annual spud growing rituals.

'To chit, or not to chit', that is the question! Pre-sprouting spuds prior to planting has been part of the potato grower's list of essential jobs-to-do throughout the long and glorious history of this most versatile of vegetables, but need it be so? A qualified 'yes' is the answer, depending on what the home producer wants to dig up for dinner.

Fast-growing First and Second Early potatoes do crop earlier and heavier if chitted. With Maincrops, which have a longer growing season before reaching maturity, chitting actually makes little difference to the final haul. However chitted Maincrop tubers will come

to maturation quicker. This is worth bearing in mind and can be a useful tactic employed by the gardener in order to beat the disastrous and devastating blight. Blight is a fungal disease which is rife across the country and can strike in warm, humid conditions anytime when conditions are right (usually from high-summer).

Individual chits can be thinned out if desired, to three or four strong, good looking ones. Generally speaking, more chits equals more spuds but smaller, whilst less chits translates to larger tatties but less (ideal if a crop of decent sized bakers is required).

HEELING IN LEEKS AND NORTH FACING CHERRIES

Leeks

Make space on the plot this week by heeling in leeks. Some of your crop might be occupying ground that'll soon be needed for other purposes. With leeks, this is no problem. They're very hardy veg, easy to move and to store. Simply lift those leeks that are in the way with a fork. Then transfer them to any handy area. Here you should have already dug out a short, 20–25 cm deep trench. Place the leeks into the trench, close together. Pack soil all around the roots and shaft. Take care not to scatter crumbs down in between the leaf folds because this'll make them gritty in the kitchen. Stored in this way, leeks will continue to stand in the ground happily and handily for many weeks.

Cherries

Morello cherry thrives in the shade so this tree is ideal for growing against a north-facing wall. It's a much sought-after sour variety, ideal for culinary use.

To train a Morello cherry as a fan against the back of a shed obtain a maiden whip from a reliable nursery and plant it during a mild spell any time between leaf-fall and bud-burst; roughly October until the end of February. Planting is not complicated. Any fairly good soil is fine. A slot made with a spade, and levered open enough to receive the roots, is perfect. To get the correct planting depth, a piece of wood can be laid over the hole. By keeping the soil mark on the tree stem level with the wood you'll ensure that your tree is not planted either too deep or too shallow. Push the fibrous roots down into the crevice with your fingers and close the soil around them gently

NATURAL HISTORY IN THE GARDEN
Lesser Celandine

One of the first flowers to appear each year is the lesser celandine. Celandines grow thickly amongst banks and hedge-bottoms and their yellow, buttercup-like flowers will be coming out in ever increasing numbers as the month passes.

In dull or wet weather the blooms close, but when the sun shines they open their little petals widely.

Celandine leaves are delicious when chopped finely with onions, parsley and herbs to make a salad dressing.

January, 5th Week

but firmly with the sole of your boot. Regular watering during the first growing season is essential.

Formative pruning at this stage involves looking closely at the whip. Aim to make a clean cut at about 45 cm with three or four healthy buds below. Fix canes either side at 45 degree angles. In the growing season, train one strong shoot to each cane. When these appear to be thriving, snip off all others. Next year, lop both back by two-thirds to a bud facing upwards. Train new growth to the cane but, additionally, allow one bud below and two above to develop. Attach to evenly spread wires. This is the beginning of your fan-trained tree.

Apart from thriving in a position where most plants would struggle, Morello is self-fertile. One tree should provide a bountiful crop for years to come.

VEGETABLE SNIPPETS
MORE LEEK FACTOIDS

Historically, it is said that Phoenician traders introduced leeks into Wales. According to legend it was 640 AD when King Cadwaller of the Britons found his men sorely pressed by invading Saxons. Cadwaller ordered his troops to wear leeks in their hats, to identify them and show whose side they were on. The Briton armies were ultimately victorious and adopted the lucky-charm leek as an emblem of national pride.

Eating leeks would also have aided these men, especially in the winter. Calcium, iron and vitamin C are all present in this vegetable. The heart benefits too, via improved blood circulation.

Jobs
to do
each
week

JOBS TO DO EACH WEEK

February, 1st Week

In the Greenhouse

- Sow leeks in trays of seed compost. Sprinkle them on to the surface like salt and pepper. Cover with 5 mm of compost shaken through a sieve. Firm gently. Keep moist but not wet.
- Sow rocket and cabbage Greyhound, Hispi F1, Filderkraut in trays. Sow seeds 3 cm apart and 1 cm deep. Handle with tweezers.
- Sow strawberry seeds, Temptation F1, Alpine in trays. Seeds are tiny. Handle with tweezers. Lightly cover with compost no more than 5 mm deep.
- Set up seed potatoes in trays to pre-sprout or 'chit'. Place in egg boxes or a tray in naturally illuminated, frost-free place. Pimples indicate where sprouts (chits) will form. Set these uppermost.

On the Plot

- Potter and tidy.
- Secure horticultural fleece over globe artichoke crowns if frost threatens.
- Clean and turn neglected corners.
- Formatively prune newly planted Morello cherry for training as a fan. Snip off at about 45 cm, flush above a bud with three other strong buds below.
- Tidy and sort out the shed.
- Construct permanent and semi-permanent paths in the veg patch.
- Make pigeon-scarers from old shredded plastic bags tied to canes.
- Secure netting over purple sprouting broccoli to keep pigeons off.
- Check over vegetables in store. Remove any showing signs of going rotten.

VEG ON THE MENU

FRESH
Salsify.
Leek.
Parsnip.
Celeriac.
Swede.
Scorzonera.
Kale.
Carrot.
Spring cabbage.
Purple sprouting.

FROM STORE
Spuds.
Beetroot.
Shallots.
Onions.
Garlic.

JOBS TO DO EACH WEEK

February, 2nd Week

In the Greenhouse

- Check seedlings. Stroke them daily to simulate the wind and make them grow physically stronger.
- Sow lettuces in trays of seed compost. Try Lobjoits Green Cos, or Salad Bowl for example. Lots to choose from. Sowing 3 cm apart and 1 cm deep is perfect. Handle with tweezers. Keep moist but not wet.
- Sow radishes French Breakfast from seed to harvest in pots. Plant 4 cm apart, 1.5 cm deep. Keep warm, moist but not wet and in good light for cropping in a few weeks.
- Plant globe artichoke seeds, one per 9 cm pot just 1.5 cm deep. Try Green Globe or other named variety.

On the Plot

- Potter and tidy. Do a little and often every time you pop up the garden.
- Hand-weed asparagus bed. Weeds must not establish here. Show them no mercy even at this time of year before it goes growing crazy!
- Cut back hedges around the plot before the nesting season for birds begins.
- Hand-weed around globe artichoke crowns. Keep nettles, dock and other perennial weeds especially at bay.
- Hand-weed around autumn-sown broad beans, rhubarb, horseradish and winter onions.
- Keep clearing and turning beds over. When the rush of spring comes you'll be glad to have the soil dug and ready in advance.

VEG ON THE MENU

FRESH

Perpetual spinach.
Jerusalem artichoke.
Celeriac.
Scorzonera.
Salsify.
Leek.
Spuds.
Kale.

FROM STORE

Onions.
Garlic.

JOBS TO DO EACH WEEK

In the Greenhouse

- Tend seedlings. Keep moist but not wet. Don't over-water! Stroke daily to strengthen stems.
- Sow turnip, White Globe, F1 Market Express in trays of seed compost. Sow 4 cm apart and 1.5 cm deep. Can be planted out later or grown to harvest as small portions in their trays. If planting out then handle with great care at that stage.

On the Plot

- Prepare a sunny bed for cucumbers; erect chicken-wire against south-facing wall for them to scramble up. Make piles 60 cm apart, each comprising one bucket of well rotted manure beneath two buckets of good garden soil.
- Potter and tidy.
- Keep clearing and turning beds.
- Hand-weed around swedes if you've any left standing and edible.

VEG ON THE MENU

FRESH
Leek.
Parsnip.
Scorzonera.
Celeriac.
Spring cabbage.
Jerusalem artichoke.
Leaf beet.

FROM STORE
Onions.
Garlic.
Squash.
Spuds.
Beetroot.

JOBS TO DO EACH WEEK

In the Greenhouse

- Tend seedlings. Keep moist but not wet and stroke them gently, daily.
- Keep on top of running repairs and maintenance jobs to gutters, seals, door hinges, glass etc.
- Purchase growing-bags. Keep them, frost-free, ready for later in the season.

On the Plot

- Make new paths with tree trunk rounds as 'stepping stones' in and around fruit trees.
- Keep harvesting Jerusalem artichokes. They're very invasive and will grow again like the clappers next season so take care to remove every last piece of tuber.
- Hand-weed here and there where crops have been harvested. A little and often is the key to keeping on top.
- Potter and tidy plot. Nurse a cup of tea or something stronger as you mosey around.
- Turn over cleaned soil. Half an hour at the time – mind your back!
- Plant broad beans, Witkiem or similar early variety, 5 cm deep at 12 cm intervals. Plant in double rows with 20 cm between each row. Protect with cloches (from the weather) or wire netting (from the crows).

VEG ON THE MENU

FRESH
Parsnip.
Swede.
Spring cabbage.
Leek.
Leaf beet.
Celeriac.
Salsify.

FROM STORE
Beetroot.
Spuds.
Squash.
Garlic.
Onions.

JOBS TO DO EACH WEEK

In the Greenhouse

- Check and tend seedlings. Stroke and keep moist but not wet.
- Sow Brussels sprout, F1 Hybrid Millenium for example, summer cabbage Hispi F1, Greyhound or Spitfire. Use peat-free multi purpose or John Innes Seed compost. Pop two seeds into a 9 cm pot, 1.5 cm deep. Remove the weakest seedling. Or start in trays, similar depth and 3 cm apart to 'prick out' into pots when seedlings are large enough to handle.
- Sow celeriac, Alablaster and Giant Prague. Seeds are tiny. Handle with tweezers. Fill a tray brim-full with compost. Bury seeds 5 mm deep. Keep moist but not wet. Celeriac germinates slowly so be patient.
- Sow pepper seeds of your chosen variety. Select for colour, size and potency. Use loam-based potting compost. Barely cover seeds in trays or pots. Keep uniformly moist and provide 18-21°C of heat. Shade with newspaper until shoots are showing through.
- Sow Sugar Snap peas in 9 cm pots. Pop in one per pot, 4 cm deep.
- Sow trays of leeks, Axima and Mammoth for example. Sprinkle them on to the surface like salt and pepper. Cover with 5 mm of compost shaken through a sieve. Firm gently. Keep moist but not wet.

On the Plot

- Harvest the last Jerusalems. Rummage through with a garden fork to unearth any overlooked pieces, then flop down a bucket or three of compost or manure to dig in later.
- Keep cleaning and turning areas as crops are harvested.
- Prepare a bed for future parsnips by turning and raking in a 'top-dressing' of dry wood ash to a fine tilth.
- Sow parsnip seeds (eg Excalibur, White King) if the soil is pleasantly mild to the touch. Sow in shallow grooves, or 'drills', 1.5 cm deep. If sowing more than one row allow 30-40 cm between. Parsnip seeds are like confetti so do it on a calm day!
- Turn and rake proposed onion bed. Tread over it lightly. Rake and re-rake.
- Sow radish, French Breakfast. Sow in weed-free soil in rows about 25 cm apart. Make drills, flood with water and allow to drain. Then place seeds individually 2.5 cm apart, cover and firm with the back of your rake.

JOBS TO DO EACH WEEK

March, 2nd Week

In the Greenhouse

- Check and tend seedlings. Stroke daily and water to keep moist but not wet.
- Sow winter cabbages (eg Ormskirk Savoy, January King), lettuces of your choice, rocket, kohlrabi, Swiss chard and leaf beet. All can go 1.5 cm deep into small pots of multi-purpose or seed compost. Or use trays at 3 cm apart to prick out when large enough to handle.
- Sow nasturtiums in trays for planting out later as described above.

On the Plot

- Sow spring onions. Make 1.5 cm deep drills and sprinkle seeds thinly into this. Cover and firm gently. There'll be no need for subsequent thinning if sprinkled sparingly. If sowing more than one row, allow 15 cm between rows.
- Sow summer radishes of your choice. Cherry Belle can be a beauty! Sow seeds at 2.5 cm intervals in 1.5 cm deep drills. Cover, firm, keep moist.
- Sow Rainbow or other varieties of chard, 2.5 cm deep in drills 30 cm apart will suffice.
- Sow Early varieties of carrots outdoors only if it's mild. Otherwise wait for more clement conditions. Rake fertile ground to a fine tilth. Do not add any fertilisers or manure. 1.5 cm deep in drills up to 30 cm apart is perfect.
- Prepare ground for long-rooted scorzonera and salsify by digging deeply.
- Continue to rake and re-rake onion beds prior to planting.
- Plant onion sets in the middle of this month. Mark rows with string tied tight between two canes, 30 cm apart. Make shallow nests with your finger at 10-15 cm intervals, then firm one each in to these. Take care not to damage the miniature onion as you snuggle them down. Check daily and re-firm any which become dislodged (by birds, cats or their sprouting roots).
- Prune-back White Filbert trees planted as bare rooters. Reduce to half their size. Cut flush above a strong bud.
- Tidy, potter and prepare the plot.
- Dig trenches one spit deep for new potatoes, and line with well-rotted manure. These varieties are collectively called First Earlies eg Aaron Pilot, Dunluce, Foremost. Calculate for 30 cm between each tuber in rows that are 60 cm apart.
- Harden-off summer cabbages and turnips. Put them outside in the day then back under cover at night for a week to ten days.

JOBS TO DO EACH WEEK

March, 3rd Week

In the Greenhouse

- Sow tomatoes in trays of seed compost (for pricking out later) or small 9 cm pots. Lightly cover seeds and keep at 18-21°C. There are loads of varieties to choose from to cultivate in a greenhouse, outdoors or in containers. Read seed packet blurb carefully and select those that best suit your needs.
- Sow Spirit of the Four Seasons lettuce. Plant seeds in trays, 3 cm apart and 1.5 cm deep. Keep moist but not wet.
- Sow Brussels sprouts as above. Wellington F1 is a great variety to try and will reliably produce generous portions for deep winter feasts.
- Check and tend seedlings.

On the Plot

- Plant out First Early potatoes. Pop each pre-sprouted ('chitted') tuber in 15 cm deep at 30 cm intervals.
- Check over onion sets daily and re-plant any dislodged by disturbance or pushed out by their own sprouting roots.
- Dig up any remaining mature leeks and store close to the kitchen by 'heeling-in'.
- Plant out summer cabbages. Dig holes 60 cm apart in rows or blocks. Flood with water, allow to drain, then enrich with a generous dollop of well-rotted manure. Plant cabbages firmly and deeply up to their first set of leaves. Fit collars to thwart 'the fly'.
- Remove bracken, straw and twigs from around globe artichoke crowns (applied as winter protection).
- Dig up and store remaining scorzonera roots in boxes of slightly moist compost.
- Prepare seed beds for future outdoor sowings. Remove all weeds, turn soil over, rake to a level, tread lightly then rake again to reduce surface to a fine tilth.
- Sow Early and Maincrop varieties of carrot in rows, 1.5 cm deep with 30 cm between rows.
- Sow parsnips when the soil is warm. Sow in shallow grooves, or 'drills', 1.5 cm deep. If sowing more than one row allow 30–40 cm between. Parsnip seeds are like confetti so do it on a calm day!
- Plant out turnip seedlings or sow direct, 1.5 cm deep, in rows 30 cm apart. Keep consistently moist to thwart leaf nibbling flea beetles. Purple Top Milan, Arcoat and White Globe are favourites.
- Top-dress potatoes with dry wood ash, if available. This simply means sprinkling it over as a light dusting and letting the rain wash it in.

JOBS TO DO EACH WEEK

March, 4th Week

In the Greenhouse

- Sow Giant Single sunflower seeds in 9 cm pots. Use a loam-based compost. Snuggle seeds in to a depth of 1.5 cm, one per pot. Keep moist but not wet. They'll germinate swiftly. Beware slugs and snails - they love sunflower seedlings.
- Sow winter varieties of cabbage such as January King (but there are loads of others so shop around), 1.5 cm deep in pots, as described for sunflowers above. Or start them in trays, 3 cm apart, to lift and transplant into pots when they're large enough to handle comfortably.
- Check moisture require-ments of seedlings. Stroke them daily to strengthen them. Remove molluscs from your greenhouse or tunnel by torchlight after dark.

On the Plot

- Clear away the last parsnips and salsify. 'Clamp' in the garden close to the kitchen (just dig a shallow hole, bung them in this and cover until needed for use).
- Remove spent Perpetual spinach plants to the compost heap.
- Dig trenches for Second Early (eg Kestrel) and Maincrop (eg Sarpo Mira) varieties of potato. Calculate for 38 cm between individual tubers in the row, 60 cm between rows for Second Earlies, but allow 75 cm for your Maincrops.
- Sow kohlrabi seeds 1.5 cm deep in short rows, every fortnight until July, for a succession of swollen, golf-ball sized, cabbage-flavoured stems.
- Split garlic bulbs and plant individual cloves about 5 cm deep and 12.5 cm apart in blocks. If planting in rows, run them parallel about 30 cm apart.
- Dig up and lift any remaining parsnips and swedes. Use them in soups.
- Sprinkle pot marigold seeds along the edge of your veg plot and rake them in. A colourful, wildlife friendly border will grow effortlessly. Flowers and young leaves are edible in salads too.
- Plant out lettuce seedlings. A sunny bed is best at this stage for swift development. 20 cm between will give your charges ample room to grow.
- Sow beetroot. Again, varieties are many and vaired. Detroit and Boltardy are reliable customers. Pop the knobbly clusters into rows 2.5 cm deep. Aim for one seed every 2 cm. Allow 30 cm betwixt rows.

JOBS TO DO EACH WEEK

March, 5th Week

In the Greenhouse

- Sow aubergine seeds. I like Long Tom but there are plenty to select from. They're not all purple either! Sow 5 mm deep in trays for future pricking out into 9 cm pots. They need warmth; 18-21°C will suffice.
- Check over your seedlings. Keep moist but not wet, monitor pests and diseases and (importantly) stroke them daily to help them to develop stem strength.
- Maintain supplies of seed and potting compost. It's a pain to run out midway through a job so get bags into the greenhouse in advance.
- Pot on rocket. Give them more space to grow by knocking them out of tight little pots, roots and compost intact, and nestling them into bigger containers with a lining of fresh growing medium.
- Do the same with other seedlings if they're growing roots out of the drainage holes in their pot bottoms.

On the Plot

- Hand-weed shallots planted on or around the Winter Solstice and top-dress with dry wood ash.
- Check over all your growing areas with a caretakers eye.
- Mulch autumn-sown garlic with fresh grass clippings to conserve moisture.
- Sow salsify and scorzonera seeds. They're long, slightly banana shaped and easy to handle as individuals. 'Station sow' by planting four seeds together 2 cm deep at 15 cm intervals. Or sow thinly in a row. Less thinning as they develop will result in more but smaller roots, but that might suit your needs better.
- Prepare seed beds by clearing, turning and raking.
- Sow carrots in to pleasantly warm soil, 1.5 cm deep in rows up to 30 cm apart.
- Sow leaf beet 2.5 cm deep in drills 30 cm apart. Pre-water the drill if weather is dry – flood with water and allow to drain before sowing.
- Harden-off leeks and cabbages. Do this by placing them outside in the day time and back indoors at night. Or, drape horticultural fleece over them at night instead (remove it daytime).
- Gather supplies of bean poles. Either purchase bamboo or harvest some hazel or ash poles from the woods.
- Plant leek seedlings in to their nursery if they were hardened-off early. Make 5 cm deep holes in moist soil with a stick or pencil. Drop one seedling per hole. Trim over-long roots if they're too straggly. Don't let roots stick out of the top. Water well to settle them down.

JOBS TO DO EACH WEEK

In the Greenhouse

- Sow more seeds of salads. Try some of the mustardy Oriental types. Follow the instructions on the packets. They should tell you all you need to know to succeed.
- Sow lettuce varieties of your choice (eg Salad Bowl, Tom Thumb) 1.5 cm deep and 3 cm apart in trays.
- Sow squash seeds. Loads of different varieties are now on offer. Select according to shape, colour, habit of growth, storage potential and taste. Insert one seed on its side per 9 cm pot of compost to a depth of 2.5 cm. Keep moist but not wet and in the shelter of an unheated greenhouse or well illuminated window-sill.
- Look over seedlings daily.
- Pot-on Giant Single sunflowers into larger containers once roots are showing from the bottom drainage holes. Get them out intact by putting your palm over the top with stem cushioned between two fingers, invert pot and tap the bottom. Root-ball should slip out nicely. Nestle this in to larger pot prepared with fresh multi-purpose or John Innes Number 2 compost.
- Pot-on Brussels sprouts plants in a similar fashion. With all the cabbage family, they can go in deep – right up to the first set of leaves.

On the Plot

- Put lettuce, cabbage and rocket seedlings outside in the daytime to harden-off. Remember to cover them with horticultural fleece, or place them back indoors, at night. Do this for a week to ten days to physically toughen up your charges.
- Hand-weed the broad beans.
- Check over all areas and crops, daily if possible.
- Cut tops off any remaining spring cabbages. Eat these as delicious 'greens'. Cut cross slits in the stump top to encourage new tufts of growth which can be eaten too. You won't get huge portions but what does grow will taste lovely!
- Plant Second Early potatoes, 15 cm deep at 38 cm intervals in rows 60 cm apart is about right.
- Hoe when the soil surface is dry. If you can exercise this weed controlling tool on a sunny morning then so much the better.
- Thin carrots. Tease out individually or in bunches if sowed too thickly. Aim for a single line of tiny carrots. Preferably do this on a dull day. Firm loosened soil and bury thinnings in the middle of your compost heap to avoid attracting pests.

JOBS TO DO EACH WEEK

April, 2nd Week

In the Greenhouse

- Sow peas, sweetcorn, dwarf French beans, squashes, courgettes, marrows, and cucumbers in pots; 2.5 cm deep is perfect.
- Sow summer cabbages and lettuces in trays or pots, 1.5 cm deep.
- Sow tomatoes in pots. With 18–21°C they should germinate well. Keep in good light and don't over heat to avoid pale and drawn ('leggy') specimens.
- Prick-out strawberry seedlings in to pots.
- Pot-on Brussels sprouts to bigger containers to give roots room to grow. Knock from their pots occasionally to look. Constricted roots, wound around the inside of the pot, are bad for your plant. Get it into a large receptacle before this happens!
- Keep seedlings moist but not wet.
- Keep greenhouse well ventilated.

On the Plot

- Put potted citrus trees (lemon and lime) outside in the sunniest place possible.
- Keep all crops moist.
- Plant out lettuce All-Year-Round and Talia at 20 cm intervals in rows 30 cm apart.
- Trim plot edges to keep them tidy.
- Remove invading couch and other grasses from the comfrey patch. Pick through by hand or with a hand fork.
- Erect rows and wigwams of hazel twigs for peas in pots to climb up.
- Sow carrots in pre-moistened, 1.5 cm deep, drills.
- Sow turnips and radishes similarly.
- Dig out any overlooked spuds from last year that are sprouting as weeds. These 'volunteers' can carry diseases over from a previous crop so should not be tolerated although, if you're desperate and prepared to risk it, you can nurture them and should get a half-decent crop.
- Dig trench for Pink Fir Apple salad potatoes. Make it a 'spit' deep (20 cm) and line with quality compost or well-rotted manure.
- Plant out rocket; 20 cm or closer will do. Everything, leaves, stalks and flowers, is edible so pick frequently. Water regularly to keep plants tender and fresh.
- Hoe winter onions.
- Hand-weed Maincrop onion sets recently planted.
- Make your own fertiliser: stuff an old wormery choc-full with nettles and comfrey after straining all remaining juice into bottles for liquid fertiliser and emptying old contents onto the plot as a mulch for fruit trees.
- Plant out summer cabbages at 45 cm spacing. Plant firmly and in fertile ground (add organic matter if possible), deep (up to first set of leaves) and fit a collar to thwart 'the fly'.

JOBS TO DO EACH WEEK

In the Greenhouse

- Plant runner beans in pots. One seed per 9 cm pot will get them going in the protected environment. Plant 4 cm deep into peat-free multi purpose compost and keep moist but not wet.
- Do the same with dwarf and climbing French beans. Keep indoors until mid May then harden off and plant out.
- Pot-on Alpine strawberries and Temptation F1 sown early February.
- Start to prick out tomato seedlings into 9 cm pots. Use John Innes Number 1 or peat-free alternative.
- Now it's a bit warmer, sow aubergines if earlier attempts failed to impress. Nestle seeds 1 cm deep in trays for pricking out later or sow two seeds per 9 cm pot and remove the weaker of the two when they come up.

On the Plot

- Plant asparagus crowns. Soak crowns in a bucket of water while you dig a trench 30 cm wide and deep. Then make a mound down the middle of the trench. Spread crowns onto this ridge at 40 cm spacing with roots either side. Cover with 12.5 cm of soil. Do nothing else except keep weed free.
- Plant out leaf beet and Swiss chard at 30–45 cm intervals.
- Cut back encroaching brambles from soft fruit bushes.
- Thin salsify and scorzonera seedlings.
- Keep on weeding by hand and hoe.
- Potter about and enjoy this fantastic time of the year!
- Plant out summer cabbages at 45 cm intervals. Plant firm and deep on top of quality compost or manure and fit a collar around the stem to thwart cabbage root flies.
- Plant out Brussels sprouts in similar fashion at 60 cm intervals. The ground must be as firm as possible to keep roots well anchored and prevent sprouts from blowing open instead of staying tightly shut.
- Dig up rogue spuds as they appear in unwanted places.
- Sow beetroot, spring onion, radish and carrot as per instructions on the seed packet.
- Plant out peas sown at the end of March. Nestle them into fertile soil with minimum disturbance to the roots. Insert supporting hazel twigs or netting to scramble up after planting out.
- Sow American land cress and/or corn salad. Sprinkle seeds down as if feeding chickens then rake in to the soil surface.

JOBS TO DO EACH WEEK

April, 4th Week

In the Greenhouse

- Sow winter cabbages such as January King and Ormskirk Savoy. Sow in trays, 1.5 cm deep and 3 cm apart to prick out when large enough to handle or in pairs in 9 cm pots (remove the weakest subsequently).
- Sow Brussels sprouts in exactly the same way.
- Pot-on tomatoes. Invert their small pots and tap the bottom. Compost and roots should slip out easily as one. Nestle into bigger pots with extra John Innes Number 2 or peat-free alternative.
- Tend all seedlings and young plants. Keep moist but not wet and ensure adequate ventilation.
- Sow bean seeds as described last week.

On the Plot

- Hand-weed asparagus bed. Yes! Do it regularly and it remains really quick and easy.
- Mulch autumn-sown Aquadulce broad beans with grass mowings.
- Plant out winter cabbages, January King and Ormskirk Savoy sown earlier in the year. Fit with collars to dissuade the cabbage root fly.
- Weed amongst the seedlings.
- Re-sow parsnips if germination has been patchy. You can do this as late as mid May quite happily. Choose a still day and take out 1.5 cm deep drill in weed-free soil. Moisten it with water dribbled from a can and allow to drain. Then sprinkle fresh seeds into this ('snip seeds don't keep for very long, unlike some veggies).
- Plant your Maincrop potatoes into prepared, enriched trenches, 15 cm deep at 38 cm intervals in rows 75 cm apart.
- Sow dwarf French beans direct. Two seeds every 20 cm and 2.5 cm deep is good. If sowing more than one row allow 45 cm between rows.
- Sow some more broad beans to extend the cropping season. Try a variety like Bunyard's Exhibition. Prepare double rows running parallel 20 cm apart. Plant seeds 5 cm deep at 12 cm intervals.
- Take a delivery of straw for mulching marrows, courgettes and squashes later in the season.
- Check over all crops regularly.
- Finish planting out salad potatoes such as Pink Fir Apple and Ratte, as for Maincrops (see above).
- Plant out leeks into a nursery bed.
- Plant out Giant Single sunflowers at 30 cm apart.
- Sow Florence fennel in a warm position. Sow seeds evenly and thinly, 1 cm deep in rows 30 cm apart.

JOBS TO DO EACH WEEK

May, 1st Week

In the Greenhouse

- Sow a deep tray full of Hurst Greenshaft peas, 4–5 cm below the surface, to plant out individually when they're about 5 cm tall. Don't be afraid to pack 'em in tight. They'll transplant fine as long as you are gentle with their roots.
- Sow purple sprouting broccoli Late in trays or pots 1.5 cm deep.
- Plant sweetcorn varieties. It's hard to believe those shrivelled little niblets will do anything but be assured – they will! One seed per 9 cm pot, 2 cm deep will suffice. Use John Innes Seed or peat-free alternative as compost. Keep it moist but not wet.

On the Plot

- Sow swedes in rows between ripening winter onions. They'll benefit from the shelter, hidden from the bead eyes of pigeons as they germinate and pop up. Either sow in 1.5 cm deep drills or 'station sow' four seeds every 10 cm or so, then remove all but the strongest from each clump. If sowing into an empty seedbed allow 30–45 cm between rows.
- Check over all crops with a caretaker's eye.
- Earth-up First Early potatoes. This just involves mounding soil up around the emerging leaves. Cover them almost completely but not quite. This'll be an ongoing job so do it a little and often to keep it from getting too heavy. Employ a swan-necked hoe or, if you have neglected your duties, perhaps a small Border spade. More edible portions form in the mounds and weeds are controlled by virtue of the action itself.
- Harden-off peas and celeriac on the cusp of going into their final resting places. Place outside daytime but inside at night (or cover with horticultural fleece) for a week or so.
- Clear spent purple sprouting plants which have finished harvesting. Bash woody stems to a pulp with a lump hammer before composting to hasten the rotting process.
- Don't cut any spears from asparagus crowns which are less than 2 years old. Plants will be stronger and more prolific over the next 15 or so years if you resist the temptation to get in too quickly now (they need to build good core strength).

JOBS TO DO EACH WEEK

May, 2nd Week

In the Greenhouse

- Water and tend crops.
- Plant runner beans in pots. One bean, 4 cm deep, per 9 cm pot is perfect. Why not try a white flowered variety like White Emergo or bi-coloured such as Painted Lady for ornamental as well as edible effect?
- Harden-off earlier plantings of beans and courgettes prior to planting out (see last week).
- Keep water supplies topped up and handy. Tending to the ventilation and watering needs of your indoor charges is a daily task.

On the Plot

- Cut back and weed plot edges to keep on top of things.
- Keep paths clear of trip hazards.
- Hand-weed amongst seedling crops.
- Hand-weed asparagus.

Go on then! Cut no more than two spears from a two-year old plant.

- Keep your hoe busy.
- Plant out nasturtiums in odd places here and there. Don't be fussy about distances etc, just whack 'em in for pretty flowers and leaves later this season.
- Earth-up Second Early potatoes (see last week).
- If rain is not forthcoming then do water your seedlings. A decent soaking at the roots is better by far than a light sprinkling overhead.
- Plant out French and runner beans 20 cm apart. Do keep an eye to the forecast. These plants are tender and will be killed by frost. Get ready to swaddle with horticul-tural fleece (or a sheet) if a freezing night is forecast.
- Plant out lettuces; 20 cm distances are perfect if you're going to let them form hearts. You can plant closer if planning to just harvest individual leaves on an almost daily basis.
- Add a splosh of home-made nettle and comfrey feed to a watering can and pour over the roots of established broad beans, greens, spinach and chard. Do not feed seedlings like this – you'll kill them with kindness as the food is too rich.
- Plant out courgettes and marrows. Marrows can go amongst runner beans. Allow 60 cm between plants with a bush habit, 120 cm betwixt those that like to trail (refer to the seed packet for this information).
- Keep a close eye on your parsnips.
- Sow carrots and spring onions.
- Prepare a seedbed for beetroot. Clear all weeds, rake it level.

JOBS TO DO EACH WEEK

In the Greenhouse

- Keep crops moist but not wet.
- Still time to sow squash seeds, 2.5 cm deep into 9 cm pots.
- Plant aubergines into large pots or grow-bags.
- Ventilate every day.

On the Plot

- Thoroughly hand-weed through the parsnips.
- Water peas, beans and cucurbits (marrows, squashes, courgettes) generously if the weather is dry.
- Plant out celeriac. Allow 30–40 cm between plants for future generous crops. Don't plant too deep. Make sure the small swelling at the top of the stem (below the leaves) stands proud of the soil surface. Celeriac thrives on water so planting in a sunken drill is a good idea. Use a draw hoe to create one. Artificially applied water will be channelled into this and go to where your veg needs it the most – the roots. Leave 45 cm between rows.
- Plant out globe artichokes. Leave a metre all round. This seems excessive when plants are young and small but they'll get rather large in time and soon fill their allotted space.
- Plant out squashes that are ready at 60 cm spacing (or 120 cm if they're the sprawling types).
- Cut back your plot edges as and when…
- Liquid feed established crops.
- Give one bucket of water per newly planted fruit tree even if there has been rain. These are long-term investments and watering now is vital to their healthy establishment.
- Earth-up potatoes whenever foliage is showing above the surface more than just a little bit (see May, 1st Week).
- Carry on weeding with hand and hoe.
- Cut more nettles and comfrey to stuff into an old wormery to make liquid plant food.

JOBS TO DO EACH WEEK

In the Greenhouse

- Tend all crops.
- Water pots and grow bags daily.
- Ventilate well.

On the Plot

- Water all crops with a watering can to get water where you want it – at the roots.
- Flood the asparagus bed if it's newly planted and the weather is dry. Young crowns want to be kept moist.
- Keep paths clear and cut grass.
- Collect and/or have delivered sacks of manure for future use. Keep at least one back to flop onto your rhubarb in November.
- Plant out later sowings of peas in rows with twiggy support or netting 5–10 cm apart.
- Plant out squashes and marrows. Afford 60 cm between plants which bush or 120 cm if they are apt to sprawl and trail.
- Earth-up potatoes.
- Hand-weed and hoe a bit every day if possible. Hoe before you can see the weeds, not after they've created a mat of green!
- Sow lettuce seeds direct into moist drills 1.5 cm deep and 30 cm apart.
- Plant out winter cabbage, cauliflower, kale and Brussels sprouts. Remember to put them into enriched soil that is moist and plant deep – up to the first set of leaves. Firm soil around roots well, especially of the sprouts. In fact, it's hard to firm soil too much for these. If it's hard like iron that's what they like! Allow 60 cm between plants. Fit collars to protect from 'the fly' and erect bird scarers at the time of planting too. Pigeons can wreck a tender crop overnight.
- Primp and preen your broad beans.

VEG ON THE MENU

FRESH
Winter purslane.
Rocket.
Radish.
Lettuce.

FROM STORE
None used

JOBS TO DO EACH WEEK

May, 5th Week

In the Greenhouse

- Water all crops and seedlings, keeping moist but not wet.
- Ventilate well.
- Keep an eye out for pests and diseases.

On the Plot

- Water crops as and when they look dry on top.
- Plant out Alpine strawberries in a shady bed (around a north-facing Morello cherry is ideal). Allow up to 15 cm between individuals.
- Plant out purple sprouting broccoli plus any extra cabbages and kale. Do this as for the cabbages last week. Take the same precautions against insects and birds.
- Give a little liquid feed to the beans.
- Cut vegetation back from paths.
- Hand-weed the parsnips.
- Keep hoiking out last years potatoes which are growing as weeds

amongst this season's crops.
- Wherever seedlings are up and leaves are touching, thin them out to give a bit more space between individuals to grow. Final spacing will depend on type and variety but for now, just thin towards this goal gradually.
- Earth-up potatoes.
- Prepare a bed for leeks. Calculate for 15 cm between each plant in rows 30 cm apart. Get rid of all weeds and rake it level.
- Hoe between lines of veg at every opportunity.
- Plant out squashes in a sunny bed at 60–120 cm intervals depending on habit (bush or trailing).
- Keep an eye out for blackfly on broad beans. If you see any don't panic! Pinch out and remove the affected tips then give the ladybirds a chance to deal with them

for you. If none have come after a week to ten days and it's looking dire then spray with diluted washing-up liquid.
- Keep leek nursery moist and weed-free.
- Take time just to stand and stare. This is a wonderful time of the year!

VEG ON THE MENU

FRESH

Radish, French Breakfast and Cherry Bell.
Winter onions.
Talia and Buttercrunch Lettuce.
Carrot, Starca F1.
Globe artichoke.
Broad beans, Aquadulce.
Swiss chard.
Perpetual spinach.

FROM STORE

None used

JOBS TO DO EACH WEEK

June, 1st Week

In the Greenhouse

- Daily watering and looking over for crops in pots and grow-bags.
- Ventilate daily.

On the Plot

- Keep on watering direct by hand (to the base of crops; the roots) and hoeing.
- Finish preparing the leek bed, clearing, digging and raking to a level.
- Import bags of manure and green waste from reliable outside sources for future use.
- Tend veggies lovingly and look over as often as possible.
- Keep planting out members of the cabbage tribe (see May, 4th Week).
- If no rain is in the area, drench your potatoes. Don't use a sprinkler. Rather, flood between the rows.
- Plant-out runner beans against poles at 20 cm intervals.
- If you're going to try your tomatoes outside then plant them into the sunniest bed possible at 45 cm spacing.
- Water young fruit trees with at least one full bucket each. Pour it around their roots slowly so it has a chance to soak in and not run off.
- Thin veggies including lettuces when plants are invading the space of their neighbours with their leaves. These lettuce thinnings are beautiful to eat so don't waste 'em.
- Plant out leeks. Use a rounded-off broken spade handle to make holes 15 cm deep at 15 cm intervals. Plonk one leek in each hole then fill with water. Let it drain naturally. 'Puddle-in' like this as often as possible for the first week or so until the leeks are established. Mud will settle around the roots naturally.
- Harvest the winter onions. They're not great keepers so hang in bunches and use between now and when the Maincrops come in (August-time).
- Earth-up potatoes.

VEG ON THE MENU

FRESH

Broad beans, Aquadulce.
Winter onions.
Radish, Cherry Bell and French Breakfast.
Lettuce, Buttercrunch and Talia.
Sugar Snap peas.
Turnip, White Globe.
Rocket.
Globe artichoke.
Perpetual spinach.
Swiss chard.
Carrot.
Shallots.

FROM STORE

None used

JOBS TO DO EACH WEEK

June, 2nd Week

In the Greenhouse

- Keep all crops moist but not wet by watering daily.
- Put supporting canes or strings in place for tomatoes.
- Don't forget to ventilate adequately.

On the Plot

- Puddle-in your leeks daily this week if possible.
- Keep crops watered direct to the roots if rain is not forthcoming.
- Plant out more cucurbits; 60 cm spacing is fine.
- Harvest shallots planted on the Winter Solstice when tops have died down and conditions are dry (if you can do this on Midsummers Day then so much the better).
- Hand-weed and hoe as much as time and circumstances allow.
- Tie sunflowers to supporting poles.
- Sow radishes and kohlrabi in 1.5 cm deep drills. Keep them moist at all times to assist speedy and tender growth.

VEG ON THE MENU

FRESH
Broad beans.
Winter onions.
Lettuce, Talia and All-Year-Round.
Rocket.
Sugar Snap peas.
Globe artichoke.
Beetroot, Mona Lisa.
Lettuce, Red Merveille.
Spuds, Concorde.
Cabbage, Derby Day.
Carrot, Starca F1.

FROM STORE
None used

JOBS TO DO EACH WEEK

June, 3rd Week

In the Greenhouse

- Ventilate, tend and water daily.
- Keep an eye out for pests and diseases.

On the Plot

- Earth-up potatoes as and when needed.
- Hand-weed asparagus bed.
- Check over members of the cabbage tribe.
- Gather up harvested winter onions, tie into bunches and hang in as dry and airy a place as possible.
- Support burgeoning broad beans. Secure posts around the double rows then lash string around these.
- Insert stout stakes at an angle adjacent to Brussels sprouts. Lash their stems to these to keep secure, especially if summer storms threaten.
- Bash stakes either end of the asparagus rows and tie strings tight between these. Two lengths low down and higher up will pinch the stems and ferns and prevent them from being knocked over in high winds. This is important. Snapping and damage low down can weaken the long-term prospects of your treasured plants.
- Sow Cylindra beetroot seeds into moist 2 cm deep drills 30 cm apart.
- Hand-weed and hoe as per usual!
- Cut the tops off your Jerusalem artichokes. They'll act like a sail in strong winds. As with asparagus, damage low down can be detrimental to the harvest.
- Test the ripeness of broad beans by squeezing the plump pods to feel for bean development within.
- Mulch around courgettes and squashes with straw to preserve water and keep fruits clean.
- Keep bird scaring devices in working order, especially around the cabbage patch.

VEG ON THE MENU

FRESH

Spuds, Concorde.
Cabbage, Derby Day.
Broad beans, Aquadulce.
Turnip, F1 Market Express.
Winter onions.
Lettuce, Red Merveille, All-Year-Round, Salad Bowl, Buttercrunch.
Rocket.
Spring onion, Toga.
Kohlrabi, Patrick.
Perpetual spinach.
Rainbow chard.
Swiss chard.
Sugar Snap peas.

FROM STORE
None used

JOBS TO DO EACH WEEK

In the Greenhouse

- Cut lower leaves from tomatoes and pinch out shoots between leaf and stem (side shoots).
- Water crops daily to keep moist but not wet.

On the Plot

- Plant out late leeks, such as Giant Winter into prepared ground and puddle-in daily (see June, 1st Week).
- Water squashes, marrows and courgettes generously.
- Harvest broad beans for freezing. Then cut stems at ground level. Leave roots in the soil to decompose and slow-release locked up stores of nitrogen for follow-on leafy green crops.
- Thin swedes to approximately 25 cm spacing for big roots, or leave them closer for more but smaller crops.
- Make a fuss of your cat if rabbits are nibbling cabbages and others. Make her keen to keep guard!
- Liquid feed as many veggies as you like once a week, especially those which produce a fruit (such as courgettes and tomatoes).
- Plant out Mammoth leeks into prepared bed (see June, 1st Week), except allow 20 cm between individuals in the row.
- Target watering to the roots. Thorough soakings once a week do plants in the ground much more good than a light daily sprinkle.
- Thin recent sowings of beetroot.
- Turn over ground standing vacant after harvesting summer cabbages.
- Cut back Rainbow and Swiss chard to encourage another flush of leaves.
- Plant out White sprouting broccoli, as for cabbages (see April, 3rd Week).

VEG ON THE MENU

FRESH

Cabbage, Derby Day.
Carrot, Armetis.
Spring onions.
Turnip, F1 Market Express.
Rainbow chard.
Beetroot, Mona Lisa.
Perpetual spinach.
Rocket.
Broad beans, Witkiem.
Baby leeks, Carentan 2.
Dwarf Fench bean, Hildora.
Long Green Marrow (taken young).
Kohlrabi, Partick.
Courgette, Gold Rush.
Beetroot, Detroit 2.
Winter onions.
Spuds, Concorde.
Radar Onion.
Sugar snap peas.
Lettuce, Salad Bowl, Sandringham, Talia.
Corn salad.
Land cress.
Globe artichoke.

JOBS TO DO EACH WEEK

July, 1st Week

In the Greenhouse

- Water and give a dose of liquid comfrey and nettle feed for crops beginning to fruit.
- Carefully monitor your plants, removing unhealthy foliage and keeping environment well ventilated.

On the Plot

- Hand-weed amongst purple sprouting and kale.
- Hoe through leeks, and anywhere else regardless of whether weeds are visible or not.
- Hand-weed garlic prior to harvesting.
- Continue to puddle-in leeks if time and inclination suits.
- Keep newly planted out globe artichokes well watered in these establishing stages.
- Lift garlic and leave in the sun to ripen fully.
- Cut back nettles and comfrey. Stuff everything in the old wormery to produce liquid fertiliser.
- Give all the beans a liquid feed. One glug per watering can of water should prove a worthwhile tonic.
- Tie outdoor tomatoes to supporting canes.
- Sow dwarf French beans direct for a late crop; 4 cm deep, 20 cm apart in rows 30 cm apart is advisable.
- Sow carrot seeds Autumn King 1.5 cm deep in moist drills made 30 cm apart.
- Hand-weed asparagus bed. By now it'll be a hands and knees job!

VEG ON THE MENU

FRESH

Lettuce, All-Year-Round, Talia, Salad Bowl, Buttercrunch, Iceberg.
Rocket.
Winter onions.
Cabbage, Derby Day.
Land cress.
Turnip, F1 Market Express.
Corn salad.
Spring onions.
Carrot, Armetis.
Broad beans, Witkiem.
Spuds, Concorde.
Kohlrabi.
Beetroot, Mona Lisa and Detroit 2.
Dwarf French bean, Hildora and Purple Teepee.
Red onions.
Cucumber, Gherkin.
Sugar Snap peas.
Courgette, Black Beauty and Goldrush.
Swiss chard.
Baby leek.

JOBS TO DO EACH WEEK

July, 2nd Week

In the Greenhouse

- Water all crops daily.
- Liquid feed.
- Ventilate.

On the Plot

- Thin latest beetroot sowings.
- Compost harvested pea plants. Cut them off at ground level but leave the roots in the soil to decompose. They're full of nitrogen which is good for future crops.
- Sow lines of lettuces if the weather is not too hot (they won't germinate in extreme heat).
- Keep crops moist but not wet with water applied to the roots not leaves.
- Hand-weed the asparagus bed.
- Carry on weeding with hand and hoe.
- Clear exhausted Swiss chard plants to the compost heap.
- Apply a mulch of well-rotted manure over the bed where broad beans were in preparation for planting spring cabbage.
- Weed and clip plot edges.
- 'Summer prune' trained varieties of apples and pears. Identify side shoots over 23 cm long. Cut those coming out of a main branch down to three leaves above the cluster by the branch.
- Sow leaf beet and Swiss chard for winter and spring supplies of greens. Scatter seeds along 1 cm deep pre-moistened drill drawn out parallel with 30–45 cm between them.
- Make further sowings of spring onion, kohlrabi and turnip. Follow the advice given on the seed packets.
- Thoroughly drench all crops in pots at least once a week.
- Keep developing globe artichoke crowns weed-fee.
- Start regular inspections of cabbages and their relations for the eggs of butterflies. Rub them out with your thumb where found.

VEG ON THE MENU

FRESH

Spuds, Concorde.
Globe artichoke.
Swiss chard.
Broad beans, Witkiem.
Lettuce, Talia, Salad Bowl, Iceberg, Buttercrunch.
Cucumber, Gherkin.
Dwarf French bean, Hildora and Purple Teepee.
Rainbow chard.
Sugar Snap peas.
Beetroot, Detriot 2.
Winter (Radar) onions.
Cabbage, Greyhound.
Radish, French Breakfast.
Land cress.
Corn salad.
Rocket.

JOBS TO DO EACH WEEK

July, 3rd Week

In the Greenhouse
- Water daily.
- Liquid feed once a week.
- Inspect all crops for pests and diseases.

On the Plot
- Keep up the watering direct to plant roots, especially cucurbits, beans, globe artichokes, asparagus and rhubarb.
- Collect grass mowings wherever possible. Add them to the compost heap or put them on the soil surface as a mulch around crops. Avoid any grass which has been treated with any kind of weedkillers for obvious reasons.
- Take badger precautions if they are in your area at night by spraying urine around their favourite nibbles (sweetcorn, carrots, parsnips, potatoes in more or less that order).
- Keep your hoe busy.
- Keep edges trimmed and weeded.
- Cut down the leaves, or 'haulm', of any potatoes showing signs of blight and burn immediately.
- Clear lettuces going to seed.

VEG ON THE MENU

FRESH
Beetroot, Mona Lisa.
Spuds, Concorde.
Cucumber, Marketmore.
Lettuce, Buttercrunch, Talia.
Radish, French Breakfast.
Spring onions.
Runner beans, Enorma.
Morello cherry.
Carrot.
Baby leek.
Marrow.
Courgette, Goldrush and Black Beauty.
Red onions.
Winter onions.
Shallots.
Garlic.
Globe artichoke.
Dwarf French beans, Hildora.
Beetroot, Detriot 2.

JOBS TO DO EACH WEEK

July, 4th Week

In the Greenhouse

- Water all crops daily.
- Feed tomatoes and aubergines once this week.
- Ensure adequate ventilation in hot weather.

On the Plot

- Weed and hoe here and there every time you pop up to the garden.
- Burn potato tops which are blighted immediately.
- Hand-weed asparagus bed.
- Water late sowings of broad beans.
- Keep swedes moist in times of low rainfall.
- Badgers are very active this month. Protect root veg nightly spraying with human urine.
- Give squashes, courgettes and marrows plenty to drink. Pour it at the roots. Avoid splashing leaves which might then scorch in the sunshine.
- Keep the cabbage tribe moist too. They don't like getting too dry.
- Hand-weed and hoe, although you should be noticing a definite slowing down of weed growth by this time of year.

VEG ON THE MENU

FRESH

Spuds, Concorde.
Courgette, Black Beauty.
Leek, Carentan 2.
Carrot.
Runner beans.
Lettuce, Talia, Sandringham, Buttercrunch.
Cucumber, Marketmore, Gherkin.
Spring onion.
French beans, Purple Teepee, Hildora.
Radish, French Breakfast.
Swiss chard.
Beetroot.
Globe artichoke.
Red onions, Red Baron.
Squash, Sunburst.

FROM STORE

Garlic.
Winter 'Radar' onions.

JOBS TO DO EACH WEEK

In the Greenhouse
- Water all crops daily.
- Once-weekly liquid feed.
- Ventilate.

On the Plot
- Cut a third off the tops of Jerusalem artichokes to prevent wind damage.
- Remove dying foliage on globe artichokes to encourage new growth.
- Water all squashes, courgettes and marrows.
- Keep seedlings moist, but avoid watering in the hot daytime to avoid scorching tender foliage.
- Tie outdoor plum tomatoes to supporting canes, and water daily.
- Inspect the plot for badger damage.
- Hand-weed a little and often.
- Sow lettuce, Montel and Enya.
- Water beans and brassicas.
- Carefully hoe along lines of leeks, then hand-weed between the plants.
- Keep a check on ripening tomatoes! Cut off some leaves low down to allow the sunshine onto the fruit.
- Take nightly badger precautions.
- Check over all crops and water where needed.
- Pinch out rampant squash shoots to contain the bushy growth if it is smothering other veggies.
- Harvest onions if the weather is fine now but the August forecast is dodgy. Lift, tie in to bunches, and hang in a sheltered but airy place to dry. If the month is set fair onions can be left standing until early September if needs be.

VEG ON THE MENU

FRESH
Spuds, Concorde.
Runner beans.
Carrot.
Onions, Red Baron.
Beetroot, Mona Lisa.
Marrow.
Cucumber, Gherkin and Marketmore.
Courgette.
Globe artichoke.

FROM STORE
Winter onions.
Garlic.

JOBS TO DO EACH WEEK

August, 2nd Week

In the Greenhouse

- Check all crops for pests and diseases.
- Water all crops daily, and feed at end of the week.

On the Plot

- Hoe and weed whenever possible wherever unwanted growth is showing.
- Keep a sharp eye on Second Early and Maincrop spuds for signs of blight. Cut down and burn haulms if necessary.
- Badger precautions each evening.
- Plant out Red Drumhead cabbages into enriched, prepared ground (see April, 3rd Week).
- Plant out Pixie cabbages.
- Secure horticultural fleece over cabbages to keep off butterflies.
- Remove small globe artichoke heads that won't be useable but will sap energy from the plant.
- Water as and when desired.
- Start to clean weeds from potato patch, and commence harvesting of Second Earlies. Wash carefully and allow to fully dry in the sun before putting into store.
- Keep up watering outdoor tomatoes.
- Fertilise sweetcorn when flowers and tassels are showing by tapping the plants to release the pollen. Do this job daily, morning and night.

VEG ON THE MENU

FRESH

Runner beans.
Spuds, Concorde.
Carrot.
Globe artichoke.
Cucumber, Gherkin.
Tomato.
Broad beans.
Dwarf French beans.
Beetroot.
Red onions.
Courgette, Black Beauty.
Swiss chard.
Aubergine.
Baby leek.

FROM STORE

Winter 'Radar' onions.
Garlic.

JOBS TO DO EACH WEEK

In the Greenhouse
- Water crops daily.
- Pick tomatoes as they come into ripeness.

On the Plot
- Dig, clean, dry and store Second Early potatoes.
- Water all crops in containers daily.
- Hoe and weed as desired.
- Continue to weed the rows of cut-down spuds before harvesting.
- Remove tatty lower leaves on celeriac.
- Tidy and potter round the plot to keep everything shipshape.
- Cut down Swiss chard and leaf beet going to seed.
- Thin lettuce seedlings, and use thinnings either to plant elsewhere or enjoy as baby leaf salad.
- Keep the hoe busy in the mornings.
- Clear away pea sticks no longer in use.

VEG ON THE MENU

FRESH
Runner beans.
Spuds, Concorde and Kestrel.
Tomatoes.
Lettuce, Sandringham.
Cucumber.
Broad beans.
Onions.
Spring onions.
Aubergine.
Sweet peppers.
Courgette.
Red onions.
Perpetual spinach.
Florence fennel, Zefa Fino.
Rainbow chard.
Carrot.

FROM STORE
Garlic.
Winter 'Radar' onions.

JOBS TO DO EACH WEEK

August, 4th Week

In the Greenhouse

- Keep providing adequate ventilation in hot weather.
- Water daily.
- Liquid feed twice this week for veggies producing a crop.

On the Plot

- Tidy the shed in preparation for veg as produce comes in to store.
- Hang dried and bunched Maincrop onions in a cool, airy shed.
- Commence to dig Maincrop potatoes (can be delayed as late as end of September if there is no blight and top growth is looking healthy).
- Allow spuds to dry in the sun for a day after washing.
- Hand-weed asparagus bed.
- Burn any diseased tomato plants immediately.
- Cut nettles around compost heaps to allow easy access.
- Trim plot edges to maintain a tidy work space.
- Weed and hoe around leeks, brassicas and parsnips.
- Clean rows of Cylindra beetroot.
- Collect seeds of favourite flowers such as pot marigold, corn cockle, black knapweed, foxglove and great mullien in paper bags under dry conditions.
- Remove tiny globe artichoke heads which won't be eaten.
- Cut off any flowers shooting from salsify and scorzonera plants.
- Start to dig salad potatoes, Pink Fir Apple.

VEG ON THE MENU

FRESH

Outdoor tomatoes.
Spuds, Concorde, Kestrel and Cara.
Broad beans.
Courgette.
Cucumber.
Florence fennel, Zefa Fino.
Sweet peppers.
Aubergine.
Marrow.
Runner beans.
Red onions.
Land cress.
Beetroot.
Perpetual spinach (leaf beet).

FROM STORE

Winter onions.
Garlic.

JOBS TO DO EACH WEEK

In the Greenhouse

- Water crops daily.
- Twice weekly liquid feed for all.
- Remove leaves from tomatoes that are shading fruits.
- Keep an eye for pests and disease, react accordingly.

On the Plot

- Dig, wash, dry and store Maincrop potatoes. Handle them gently so as not to damage their skins.
- On the salad potatoes, remove the foliage, weed completely and commence to lift, wash, dry and store these too.
- Prune Morello cherry that has fruited: snip out branches that bore the cherries and tie in this season's growth that is fresh, young and fit to bear next summer.
- Tie-in branches of trained apples to the supporting wires.
- Water all veggies in containers. Give them a good drench.
- Sling some well-rotted manure down where the potatoes were, fork it in to the soil and rake level.
- Prepare a bed for winter Radar onions by sprinkling wood ash, raking the surface to a crumbly tilth, treading firm with sideways tick-tack footsteps (the so-called 'Gardeners Shuffle') and then repeating the process once more.
- Water and weed where needed, especially the beans.
- Hoe open soil to keep weeds in check. Broadcast-sow a green manure if this particular plot isn't needed for a few months.
- Tickle around the strawberries, weeding and removing dead leaves. This is the time to plant new specimens.

VEG ON THE MENU

FRESH
Squash, Sunburst.
Florence fennel.
Aubergine.
Marrow.
Green peppers.
Leaf beet.
Sweet pepper.
Beetroot.
Strawberry.
Courgette.
Carrot.
Broad beans.
Runner beans.
Tomatoes.
Leek, Carentan 2.
Cucumber.
Spring onions.
Rocket.
Lettuce.
Pink Fir Apple potato.
Globe artichoke.

FROM STORE
Red onions.
Garlic.
Spuds, Kestrel and Cara.

JOBS TO DO EACH WEEK

September, 1st Week

In the Greenhouse

- Carefully clear spent plants showing signs of disease such as grey mould (botrytis).
- Water peppers and aubergines daily.
- Ensure adequate ventilation.
- Water tomatoes every two or three days.
- Empty spent pots and growbags onto the garden.
- Sow a tray of winter purslane (miners' lettuce). Handle tiny seeds with tweezers. Sow in a tray of moist seed compost, only 2 or 3mm deep.

On the Plot

- Plant winter Radar onion sets. Firm acorn-sized sets in lines at 10–15 cm intervals. Allow 30 cm between parallel lines.
- Continue to dig, wash, dry and store salad and Maincrop potatoes.
- Apply a goodly dose of water to the roots of squashes.
- Liquid feed celeriac.
- Tidy fattening celeriac. Remove the tatty lower leaves. Tug downwards and to the side sharply and they'll come away neatly. Why bother? Well, it makes them look handsome and removes slug and snail hidey-holes.
- Put all grass mowings on the compost heap.
- Water all crops, especially the cabbage tribe.
- Collect seeds of pot marigold on a fine day. Put them in a paper bag and store for sowing next year.
- Clear encroaching vegetation from around fruit trees carefully with a hand-fork, water generously and mulch with bark chippings or well-rotted manure.
- Keep snapping leaves off outdoor tomatoes to hasten ripening of remaining fruits.
- Check your cabbages and relations every other evening for butterfly eggs and caterpillars. Crush the eggs. Remove caterpillars to a sacrificial crop of nasturtiums cultivated especially elsewhere.
- Deposit leafmould and compost onto the plot in piles ready for spreading in the winter.
- Pull and compost spent rocket.
- When runner beans have finished cropping cut them at ground level and compost all the tops. Leave the roots to rot down naturally. Look for dry pods of beans to save for next year.

JOBS TO DO EACH WEEK

In the Greenhouse

- Keep watering tomatoes, peppers, aubergines and other sparingly.
- Ensure newly sown seeds are kept moist.
- Sow lettuce, Winter Density and All-Year-Round. Sow seeds 1.5 cm deep and 3 cm apart in trays of moist seed compost.
- Remove plants as they are spent. Burn them (don't compost) to avoid spreading diseases, to which tomatoes in particular are prone.

On the Plot

- Check everything.
- Put up shredded plastic bags on sticks to deter pigeons around the cabbages and their cousins, including swedes.
- Collect and deliver tree leaves from wherever they can be easily gathered. Deposit in bins or contained piles.
- Keep the hoe busy between standing crops.
- Hand-weed the asparagus.
- Keep harvesting courgettes, marrows and beans (if you're lucky).
- Cut back plot edges and paths.
- Mulch kale with mature manure.
- Check the cabbage tribe for butterfly eggs and caterpillars.
- Tie purple sprouting broccoli plants to stout stakes to keep them firmly in place in the face of winter storms.
- Cut back encroaching brambles.
- Thoroughly clean soil where crops have been harvested and sow with a green manure such as Phacelia or Field beans if not needed for immediate use.
- Carry on lifting and preparing potatoes for storage (see August, 5th Week).
- Harvest your squashes. Don't just slice them off. Rather, carefully cut either side of where the stem joins the vine, to create a T-shape. They'll store for longer like this.
- Tie the Maincrop onion haul into bunches and hang these in a cool, dry and airy place.

JOBS TO DO EACH WEEK

September, 3rd Week

In the Greenhouse

- Water remaining fruitful crops every three days.
- Clear spent plants and growing medium.
- Keep seedlings moist but not wet.
- Don't forget to ventilate the greenhouse!

On the Plot

- Lift fleece which is covering members of the cabbage tribe and protecting them from butterflies and pigeons, crawl underneath to do some weeding, then replace.
- Empty contents of the compost bin at strategic points on the plot for future use.
- Continue to collect grass mowings and put them on the working compost heap.
- Hoe through recently planted winter onions, parsnips and leeks.
- Clear squash plants once the fruits have been harvested. Chuck them on the compost heap.
- Burn the remains of outdoor tomatoes instead of composting as they often have fungal diseases by now. If you compost them the fungus will likely be passed on to future crops in the compost itself.
- Strip off the outside leaves from Swiss chard and perpetual spinach (leaf beet) to encourage the sprouting of new, fresh growth.
- Sow corn salad in odd corners. Literally just sprinkle the seeds onto bare soil and rake them in to the surface layer. This diminutive plant is quite hardy and will give you early garnish for dishes in the 'Hungry Gap' next spring.
- Maintain order in the shed!
- Regularly look over and sniff stored vegetables and fruit (especially potatoes).

VEG ON THE MENU

FRESH
Strawberry.
Tomatoes.
Aubergine.
Okra.
Sweet red and green peppers.
Courgette, Goldrush.
Florence fennel.
Sunburst squash.
Carrot.
Leaf beet.
Grape.
Beetroot.
Cucumber.
Nottingham cobnut.
Swiss chard.

FROM STORE
Onions.
Garlic.
Red onions.
Spuds.

JOBS TO DO EACH WEEK

In the Greenhouse

- Keep seedlings moist.
- Remove and burn spent tomato and pepper plants.
- Keep watering anything which continues to be productive every second or third day. Keep seedlings moist but not wet.
- Ventilate.

On the Plot

- Check potatoes in store, remove any bad ones.
- Continue to apply as much bulky organic matter (manure, molehills, leafmould, compost) to the plot as can be spared.
- Potter about and enjoy the mellow fruitfulness of autumn.
- Weed the ground where squashes were and turn the soil afterwards.
- Weed plot edges, especially removing the invasive white wiry 'boot laces' of couch grass.
- Hand-weed your winter onions to get the rows really clean.
- Cut off flower heads on globe artichokes and remove tatty foliage.
- Compost dead and dying rhubarb stalks. They'll come away with barely any encouragement when ready for recycling.
- Turn over a portion of ground in preparation for winter lettuces and other cold season Oriental salads.
- Tidy away odds and ends, especially the bits of plastic which inevitably litter the place these days.
- Sow a green manure on any soil which will be left uncultivated over winter. At this time of year Field beans and Perennial rye are your best options. Scatter them around and rake in (or otherwise do as told on the seed packets).

VEG ON THE MENU

FRESH

Courgette, Black Beauty and Goldrush.
Onion.
Sweet peppers.
Carrot.
Beetroot.
Lettuce.
Leek, Axima.
Turnip, Purple Top Milan.

FROM STORE

Red onions.
Garlic.
Shallots.
Spuds, Kestrel.

JOBS TO DO EACH WEEK

In the Greenhouse

- Continue to clear crops as plants become exhausted.
- Clean the gutters of fallen leaves.
- Harvest Ring o Fire chilli's and remove spent plants.
- Tidy pots, bags and accumulated rubbish.
- At the end of the week: remove the entire greenhouse contents outside onto wooden pallets (to keep them off the soil), then clean the windows and sweep the floor. Wash the insides thoroughly with a biodegradable detergent.

On the Plot

- Keep on collecting leaves from elsewhere and depositing in a suitable pile in the garden.
- Tidy round your purple sprouting broccoli and kale by removing dead and dying lower leaves and weeding thoroughly in the vicinity.
- Stake large members of the cabbage tribe to keep them firmly rooted. Use a draw hoe to earth-up around the stems for additional support.
- Cut plot edges.
- Plant out winter purslane, All-Year-Round and Winter Density lettuces.
- Harvest Butternut squashes if not already done so (see September, 2nd Week).
- Clear previously hard working courgette plants to the compost heap.

VEG ON THE MENU

FRESH

Carrot.
Spring onions.
Lettuce.
Beetroot.
Celeriac, Giant Prague.
Cucumber.
Sweet peppers.
Tomatoes.
Swiss chard.
Leek.

FROM STORE

Red onions.
Spuds, Kestrel.
Sunburst squash.
Garlic.
Onions.

JOBS TO DO EACH WEEK

In the Greenhouse

- Carry out essential maintenance and repairs while it is empty.

On the Plot

- Check over all crops.
- Keep cleaning and turning vacant ground.
- Ensure that bird scarers on the cabbage patch are in good working order.
- Keep collecting fallen leaves and storing them in contained piles. Or, just keep them in plastic refuse sacks with a few holes pierced in the side and stashed somewhere out of the way for twelve months.
- Cover newly planted-out salads with upturned jam jars for protection against the elements.
- Sow broad beans any time between now and December. Aquadulce is the variety of choice for autumnal sowing, but you could be bold and try Imperial Green Windsor. Mark out parallel rows with string tied tight between two canes, 20 cm apart. Pop the chunky seeds in at 12 cm intervals and 8 cm deep. Protect the planting ground from crows – once they've sussed where to plunder an emerging crop they'll be back every year!
- Feast your eyes on parsnips, swedes and celeriac ready now for harvesting.

VEG ON THE MENU

FRESH

Celeriac.
Globe artichoke.
Courgette, Black Beauty.
Tomatoes.
Aubergine.
Beetroot, Cylindra.
Leek, Axima.
Swiss chard.
Turnip, Purple Top Milan.
Carrot.
Parsnip.
Swede, Marian.

FROM STORE

Butternut squash.
Red onions.
Spuds, Kestrel and Cara.
Garlic.
Onions.
Shallots.
Chilli pepper.

JOBS TO DO EACH WEEK

October, 3rd Week

In the Greenhouse

- Start to replace shelves and pots as they get washed.
- Pot-up strawberry youngsters and 'runners' which are offshoots from the parent plants.
- Pot-on salads still indoors.

On the Plot

- Tend parsnips by removing dead leaves and keeping the crowns tidy. This removes places for pests to linger.
- Pinch off any flower buds from scorzonera or salsify to concentrate their energy into those edible roots.
- Wash dirty pots at every opportunity. A little and often will get this job done. Allow to dry and replace.
- Compost spent bean plants. Save any overlooked dry seeds for next year.
- Plant blackcurrants. Most soils are fine, even slightly damp. Avoid hollows prone to frost. Allow 1.5 metres minimum between bushes. Spread roots out and snuggle soil around them.
- Prune blackcurrants between now and March. Remove dead, diseased, crossing, dying or spindly branches. Completely cut out a third of old branches, noted by darker bark, on established bushes.
- Propagate blackcurrants. Trim 25 cm lengths of strong new pencil-thick growth. Simply insert into soil. They'll root and shoot like magic. Lift and re-establish into final resting places in a year.

VEG ON THE MENU

FRESH

Swede.
Carrot.
Parsnip.
Celeriac.
Lettuce.

FROM STORE

Garlic.
Red onions.
Spuds, Kestrel and Pink Fir Apple.
Chilli peppers.
Onions.
Shallots.
Spaghetti squash.

JOBS TO DO EACH WEEK

In the Greenhouse

- Tend to plants and seedlings. Don't over water. In fact, keeping them on the dry side is better than too wet.

On the Plot

- Put tree leaves on the leafmould pile.
- Collect and store horse manure in plastic bags. Use it only when throbbing and heaving with worms.
- Cut down asparagus ferns at ground level when they have turned dry and yellow…
- … then weed the bed meticulously.
- Stake and tie White Sprouting broccoli.
- Continue to swill out dirty pots before returning them into the greenhouse.
- Tie-in branches of Morello cherry that are lolling about.
- Plant Thermidrome or other varieties of garlic to over-winter. Break the bulbs into individual cloves. Pop them in in lines or blocks, 6 cm deep, with 12.5 cm between.
- Start pruning apple and pear trees grown as bushes or standards (ie not in a restricted form). This can be done any time between now and early March. Take out dead, diseased, dying and crossing branches and twigs. Cut back young extensions to main branches by a third or a half. Snip side-shoots coming off these to three or four buds only. If there are lots of knobbly so-called 'spurs' with fat fruit buds on perhaps thin these out so there is 10–12.5 cm between each spur. Some would say leave this job until later but my experience is that bad weather to come can hamper pruning so do what you can whenever you can and that way you'll stay ahead!

VEG ON THE MENU

FRESH
Beetroot, Cylindra.
Swiss chard.
Leaf beet.
Leek, Axima.
Carrot.
Coriander.
Salsify.
Turnip, Purple Top Milan.
Celeriac.

FROM STORE
Spuds, Cara and Pink Fir Apple.
Onions.
Garlic.

JOBS TO DO EACH WEEK

JOBS TO DO EACH WEEK

November, 1st Week

In the Greenhouse

- Finish off essential maintenance jobs.
- Replace washed and disinfected pots, shelves and accessories.

On the Plot

- Cut down Jerusalem artichoke tops to just above ground level. They're in season now and ready to dig as required.
- Snip around plot edges to keep neat and tidy.
- Thoroughly weed the asparagus bed then flop a thick mulch of compost, leafmould or well-rotted manure on top and spread over the ridges.
- Tend winter onions by hand-weeding.
- Plant more garlic cloves (see October, 4th Week).
- Dig over soil where courgettes were.
- Cut back and compost the comfrey.
- Commence raking level those piles of bulky organic matter deposited here and there in the early autumn.
- Hand-weed amongst the root veg.
- Use a garden fork to weed close to the edges and remove invasive weeds including couch grass.
- Tickle a hoe amongst the cabbage patch.
- Tear off withered old leaves from celeriac.

VEG ON THE MENU

FRESH
Beetroot.
Jerusalem artichoke.
Leaf beet.
Lettuce.
Spring onions.
Carrot.
Leek, Axima.
Swede.
Parsnip.
Brussels sprouts.
Bramley apple.

FROM STORE
Spuds, Kestrel.
Red onions.
Squash.
Butternut squash.
Garlic.
Onions.

JOBS TO DO EACH WEEK

In the Greenhouse
- Check on plants.
- Ventilate if needs-be.

On the Plot
- Check all crops.
- Import more leaves from unpolluted areas.
- Store thick wooden planks somewhere handy and dry for future use as walking boards which will protect the soil.
- Mulch around fruit trees with rotted bark chippings.
- Keep a watchful caretakers' eye over the cabbage patch for caterpillars. They can still be munching merrily right through until December if mild conditions permit.
- Plant gooseberry bushes. Select a sunny, well-drained site. Enrich ground with compost or well-rotted manure. Spread roots out. Ensure specimens show 10–20 cm of clear stem ('leg') and four or five small branches. Imagine the fully-grown bush as resembling a wine glass. Allow 1.2 metres between each.
- Prune established gooseberry bushes. Reduce main stems by half. Reduce side-shoots to four or five buds. Completely cut out any shoots coming from the base.

VEG ON THE MENU

FRESH
Lettuce.
Spring onions.
Celeriac, Giant Prague.
Jerusalem artichoke.
Cauliflower.
Land cress.
Beetroot.
Carrot.
Leaf beet.
Swiss chard.
Leek.
Swede.
Scorzonera.
Brussels sprouts.
Salsify.

FROM STORE
Spuds, Kestrel and Cara.
Onions.
Garlic.
Chilli peppers.
Spaghetti squash.
Shallots.
Sunburst squash.

JOBS TO DO EACH WEEK

In the Greenhouse

- Not much to do. Just keep an eye on plants.
- Ventilate daytime if not too cold.

On the Plot

- Sprinkle lime on beds planned for brassicas. About one handful per square metre is perfect.
- Bag up and store wood ash from bonfires. Be sure to keep it in fireproof containers and dry.
- Clear encroaching undergrowth where it is not wanted for wildlife habitat.
- Check over the stored fruit and veg. Feel, look and sniff. Reject anything which is less than perfect.
- Cut down the crowns of globe artichokes. Apply a thick mulch of leafmould on top. Continue winter pruning of apples and pears (see October, 4th Week).
- Plant out potted corn salad specimens in a sunny bed with protection. A horticultural fleece or plastic bottles, with their bottoms cut off, will do the job.
- Propagate gooseberries. Ideally use 30 cm long, pencil-thick lengths removed during pruning operations last week. Nick out all buds and the biggest thorns except the top four or five. Either make a trench, line with sand and firm them into this or (on light soils) just stick 'em in. Allow 15 cm spacings in rows 45 cm apart. Ensure that the bottom buds are at least 5 cm above the soil. Lift and transplant when rooted in a year.

VEG ON THE MENU

FRESH
Carrot.
Celeriac.
Beetroot.
Leek.
Salsify.

FROM STORE
Onions.
Spuds, Kestrel.
Garlic.
Red onions.
Butternut squash.

JOBS TO DO EACH WEEK

November, 4th Week

In the Greenhouse

- Enjoy the fact that there are no pressing jobs to do!

On the Plot

- Take time to enjoy the sights and sounds of the veg patch.
- Cut down and dig-in Phacelia green manure.
- Hand weed and hoe if the weather is dry.
- Trim non-fruiting hedges which border the plot. Leave those with berries until early February. This way the birds can feast on the natural larder but trimming occurs before the nesting season commences.

VEG ON THE MENU

FRESH
Parsnip.
Leaf beet.
Cauliflower.
Celeriac.
Beetroot.
Leek, Axima.
Swede.
Scorzonera.
Kale.
Brussels sprouts.
Jerusalem artichoke.

FROM STORE
Butternut squash.
Onions.
Spuds, Pink Fir Apple and Kestrel.
Red onions.
Chilli peppers.
Shallots.
Spaghetti squash.

JOBS TO DO EACH WEEK

November, 5th Week

In the Greenhouse

- Clean up dead and dying leaves from strawberry plants.
- Ventilate.

On the Plot

- Do a bit of digging unless soil is sandy, in which case it is better to dig in the late winter/early spring.
- Sweep paths.
- Trim around the edges.
- Dig out leaf mould bin (from last year) and spread onto the plot.
- If you have the time and inclination then turn the compost heap onto its head. But honestly, it matters not if you don't.

VEG ON THE MENU

FRESH
Celeriac.
Kale, Thousandhead.
Swede.
Leek, Axima.
Salsify.
Carrot.

FROM STORE
Onions.
Garlic.
Spuds, Kestrel.

JOBS TO DO EACH WEEK

In the Greenhouse

- Sow early peas, Feltham First, in pots or crammed together in deep trays. They can be teased apart before planting outside in the early spring, 5 cm deep.
- Check on strawberry plants.
- Pot-on winter purslane so their roots don't get constricted.

On the Plot

- Clean and tidy the entrance to the greenhouse (remove trip hazards and potential accidents).
- Remove yellowing foliage from purple sprouting broccoli and other related veggies. Firm soil around their roots at the same time.
- Tear off old, outer leaves from celeriac.
- Tend carrots still in the ground by checking for rot. Don't forget to lift and eat them!
- Order up seed catalogues for pleasant winter reading!

VEG ON THE MENU

FRESH
Celeriac.
Jerusalem artichoke.
Kale, Dwarf Green Curled and Thousandhead.
Brussels sprouts.
Leek, Axima.
Swede.

FROM STORE
Spaghetti squash.
Garlic.
Onions.
Spuds, Cara.
Shallots.

JOBS TO DO EACH WEEK

In the Greenhouse

- Not a lot to do so just relax and maybe check equipment.

On the Plot

- Weed through Red Drumhead cabbages.
- Firm round red cabbages, then mulch with well-rotted manure.
- Weed as you harvest leeks.
- Sort through shallots in store and select the firmest and best-looking for replanting around mid-winter.
- Prepare bed for shallots. Remove all weeds, rake soil level, tread it firm, sprinkle wood ash if you have any, rake again.
- Work out a planting plan for next year. Do this on paper. Decide what to grow and where.

VEG ON THE MENU

FRESH
Leek, Axima.
Winter purslane.
Land cress.
Lettuce.
Spring onions.
Kale, Dwarf Green Curled, Thousandhead, Westland Winter.
Parsnip.
Swede.
Salsify.
Carrot.

FROM STORE
Onions.
Spuds.
Shallots.
Spaghetti squash.
Garlic.
Red onions.

JOBS TO DO EACH WEEK

In the Greenhouse

- Clean and disinfect pots and shelves if needs be but otherwise don't worry.

On the Plot

- Plant shallots every 23 cm in rows 30 cm apart. Nestle them in so that the top third of each bulb remains proud of the soil surface.

VEG ON THE MENU

FRESH
Celeriac.
Leek.
Carrot.
Swede.
Salsify.
Scorzonera.
Kale.
Brussels sprouts.
Lettuce.
Parsnip.

FROM STORE
Onions.
Garlic.
Spuds, Pink Fir Apple.
Beetroot pickle.
Spaghetti squash.
Onion squash.
Shallots.

JOBS TO DO EACH WEEK

On the Plot

- Plan next season's crop rotation on paper. It's not always practical to grow different crops in different places, especially if your veg patch is small, but it is best practice to avoid repeatedly cultivating the same things in the same soil year after year. If possible apply manure and/or compost: then grow the cabbage tribe; then peas beans and pods; then the onion family including leeks; then potatoes roots and tubers before manuring again.
- Apply mulch of dry bracken to globe artichoke crowns.
- Harvest Brussels sprouts for feast-time. Snap them off from the bottom of the stem working upwards.
- Sort through squashes in store. If any are going mouldy just cut off the affected areas and use the rest immediately. Roast it or make soup.

VEG ON THE MENU

FRESH
Leek, Axima.
Brussels sprouts.
Kale, Dwarf Green
Curled, Westland
Winter.
Celeriac.
Carrot, Autumn King.
Celeriac tops.
Jerusalem artichoke.
Leaf beet.
Spring onions.
Lettuce.
Winter purslane.

FROM STORE
Spuds, Cara.
Garlic.
Onions.
Shallots.
Squash.

JOBS TO DO EACH WEEK

In the Greenhouse

- Keep potted crops on the dry side rather than too wet at this cold and difficult time of year.
- Remove mouldy outer leaves from crops in pots.
- Get in supplies of compost for sowing seeds in the spring.

On the Plot

- Prepare enclosed planting hole for fig tree against a south or south-west facing shed about 76 cm x 2.3 metres. Line the bottoms and sides with slabs to restrict root growth. They'll fruit better if treated harshly. If their roots can travel freely all you'll get is a lot of leaves but not much edible.
- Check over all crops.
- Keep the cabbage tribe clean by removing yellowing or brown lower leaves.
- Compost marrows and squashes which have failed in store, but do save and dry some seeds.
- Keep digging Jerusalem artichokes.
- Dig out nettles and willowherb wherever it is not wanted.

VEG ON THE MENU

FRESH
Swiss chard.
Leaf beet.
Swede.
Leek.
Jerusalem artichoke.
Carrot.
Winter purslane.
Kale.
Cabbage, January King.
Brussels sprouts.

FROM STORE
Onions.
Garlic.
Spuds, Cara.

JOBS TO DO EACH WEEK

In the Greenhouse

- Remove yellowing leaves from strawberries.
- Set out seed potatoes to chit. Egg boxes or plastic fruit trays are good for this. Keep your potatoes in good light, frost free, and as stout little shoots develop turn them so the 'rose end' (that with most sprouts, or 'chits') is uppermost.
- Pot-on Winter Density lettuces.
- Sow tomatoes to raise in the house on a warm windowsill. They like 18–21°C best. Sow seeds 5 mm deep in trays. If you put them in your airing cupboard to start with remove immediately they germinate. Failure to do so will result in pale, drawn, leggy seedlings which will never make good specimens and you'll have to start again.

On the Plot

- Have a close-up look at catkins on cobnuts and filberts.
- Firm-in loosened shallots. It isn't just birds that pull them up as often written; cats are a menace too and sprouting roots can actually push the shallot bulb in the air if they fail to get down into the soil.
- Weed a plot for onions and fork-in compost.

VEG ON THE MENU

FRESH
Celeriac.
Winter purslane.
Brussels sprouts.
Cauliflower.
Carrot.
Parsnip.

FROM STORE
Spuds, Cara.
Shallots.
Onions.
Garlic.

JOBS TO DO EACH WEEK

In the Greenhouse

- Water seedlings.
- Check over.
- Cover chitting spuds with newspaper at night if temperatures threaten below freezing. Light a slow burning candle and cover with clay pot. That'll keep the chill slightly at bay.
- Sow cabbages, Greyhound and Hispi F1, 1.5 cm deep and 3 cm apart in trays.
- Sow lettuce, Lobjoits Green Cos, as described for cabbages above.

On the Plot

- Start to spread mature contents of the compost heap onto the garden.
- Tickle about here and there while harvesting.

VEG ON THE MENU

FRESH
Celeriac.
Jerusalem artichoke.
Leek.
Kale.
Cauliflower.
Cabbage, January King.
Scorzonera.
Corn salad.
Winter purslane.
Carrot.
Brussels sprouts.
Swiss chard.

FROM STORE
Garlic.
Onions.
Shallots.
Spuds, Pink Fir Apple and Cara.

JOBS TO DO EACH WEEK

In the Greenhouse

- Keep an eye on chitting spuds in extreme cold. Don't allow to get frost-bitten. Use the candle under clay pot tactic (see January, 3rd Week).
- Tend seedlings.

On the Plot

- Remove remains of sunflower stalks and remove to the compost heap.
- Plant garlic, Printador. See October, 4th Week for details.
- Clear remaining leeks from main bed and heel-in near the house. Just lift them up and plonk in a rough-dug trench. Pack loose soil around the stems taking care not to get too much in between the rolls of leaves.
- Dig a trench for runner beans and start to fill with green kitchen waste.
- Transplant self-sown gooseberry from veg patch to wildlife bank at the back of the plot.
- Define plot edges by digging and weeding thoroughly.

VEG ON THE MENU

FRESH
Swede.
Cauliflower.
Cabbage, January King.
Parsnip.
Scorzonera.
Winter purslane.
Leek.
Celeriac.
Salsify.
Carrot.
Kale.
Brussels sprouts.

FROM STORE
Spuds, Cara.
Onions.
Garlic.
Shallots.

Veg on the Menu

APPLES

APPLES

Apple Upside-down Cake

Method:
1. Grease the sides, inside edges and base of an 20cm baking tray with margarine.
2. Peel and core 1 or 2 eating apples (enough to cover the tray base). Slice and blanche them.
3. Sprinkle light brown or muscovado sugar on top of the slices according to how sweet your tooth is. Fill all the gaps as well as putting enough to pat down on top of the apples.
4. Pour your favourite sponge-cake recipe over the sugar and apple mixture and bake as per your sponge recipe instructions.
5. When cooked, remove from the oven and allow to cool for 10 minutes. Use a knife to go round the edges to ensure nothing has stuck. Invert onto a cake plate.
6. Eat while still warm for maximum pleasure!

Apple Crumble

Ingredients:
- 1kg 350g cooking apples such as Bramley Seedling
- 175g soft light brown sugar
- Pinch mixed spice
- Sprinkling ground almonds
- Dash of lemon juice (2 dashes even better!)
- Enough (but very little) water to avoid the apples sticking to pan. Could use undiluted orange squash instead.

Cook apples. When cold spread in a lightly greased casserole dish.

Crumble:
- 250g plain flour
- 175g margarine
- 75g caster sugar
- Dusting of dry porridge oats
- Optional: could also use ground almonds and/or ground hazelnuts in small quantities.

Method:
1. Sift the flour. Cut the margarine into small pieces and rub into the flour. Add sugar, any optional ingredients, and continue rubbing with your fingers until mixture clings together in large crumbs.
2. Cover apples with crumble, patting down slightly.
3. Cook at 200°C (400°F or Gas Mark 6) for 15 minutes then 190°C (375°F or Gas Mark 5) for a further 15 minutes until ready.

APPLES

Winter warming Apple-a-la-mode

Ingredients:
- 450g hard sweet eating apples (a variety that does not go fluffy when cooking, such as James Grieve, Egremont Russet or George Neal)
- 25g margarine
- 2 tablespoons caster sugar
- Sprinkling of ground almonds

Method:
Peel and thinly slice the apples.

Melt margarine in frying pan. Add sliced apples and sugar. Cook very gently until pale golden, sprinkle with ground almonds, turn over gently and cook for a further few minutes.

Serve hot with vanilla ice dessert.

BEANS, RUNNER OR FRENCH

Bean, Potato and Garlic Bhugia

Ingredients:
- Red chilli pod, fresh or dried
- Oil
- Jeera (ground cumin seeds)
- Garlic
- Beans
- Turmeric (haldi)
- Red chilli powder
- Salt
- Diced potatoes

Method:
1. Drizzle a generous dose of oil into a frying pan. Add 1 teaspoon cumin seeds, 2 teaspoons finely chopped garlic, broken red chilli pod complete with seeds. Fry briefly.
2. Add diced spuds and fry for 2 or 3 minutes turning frequently.
3. Add 1 teaspoon turmeric, 1 teaspoon red chilli powder, then chopped beans. Fry until spuds are cooked through on a low heat.

The term 'bhugia' means 'dry dish'. Serves best with boiled rice and a 'wet' lentil dish.

BEANS, RUNNER OR FRENCH

Beans with Baby Aubergines

Ingredients:
- Equal amounts of baby aubergines (rinsed, dried, stalks removed) and beans (chopped)
- Finger-nail sized pieces of fresh ginger, chopped
- 2 garlic cloves
- 1 onion, finely chopped
- 1 green chilli
- 3 ripe chopped tomatoes
- 1 teaspoon dried methi seeds
- Salt to taste
- Water and oil

Method:

1. Add peeled and chopped ginger and garlic to deseeded chilli. Add a drop of water and grind these ingredients into a paste.

2. Fry chopped onion until golden.

3. Add paste to the onions and fry for a further couple of minutes.

4. Combine with chopped beans and methi seeds, cooking for a further 10 minutes (keep an eye on it as extra water and / or oil may be needed to prevent sticking).

5. Cut aubergines into lengths, add to pan and cook for another 5 minutes.

6. Add chopped tomatoes and cook with a lid on at medium heat for a further 20 to 30 minutes until done.

BEETROOT

The joy of home-grown beetroot is that it is a 'double vegetable'. Although most folk only eat the plump and juicy root, the fresh and un-nibbled tops are a fantastic dish in their own right when cooked in the same manner as any other greens. Shop-bought beets are either missing the tops altogether or, if still intact, they are tired, drooping and not worth a second thought.

Boiled

Twist off the tops by hand. Cook beetroot in a lidded pot (40 minutes on a simmer after boil should suffice) or pressure cooker with a pinch of salt added to the water. If done in a pot, avoid the temptation to stick them with a fork to test whether they are done as each fork prick causes lovely red juices to run out.

When cool enough after cooking use your hands to simply 'pop' the beets out of their skins. They will shine like deep crimson marbles.

Nothing quite compares to the sight of steaming beets lavished with melting margarine oozing along the hot slices and meandering into the other items on the plate.

Pickled

Using sliced cooked beets and sliced raw onion, layer them alternately in a sterilised jar with beets at the bottom. When full add enough white or malt vinegar to cover. Put the lids on tightly and hide them away – out of sight and out of mind! Do not be tempted for at least a month. This pickle will easily last a year.

Grated Raw

Easy! Just grate a young beetroot into a bowl for a perfect accompaniment to baked potatoes.

BROAD BEANS

BROAD BEANS

Old broads need plenty of cooking and the skins are tough, so use young and tender beans for a truly wonderful culinary experience. A brief skirmish with a little boiling water in a pot for a couple of minutes should suffice.

In Salad

Cook and allow to cool; broad beans, asparagus and French beans.

Method:

Make a dressing of 1 tablespoon dried mustard powder, 2 tablespoons lemon juice, 5 tablespoons olive oil, salt and pepper to taste. Mix thoroughly and drizzle all over your three-veg dish.

Risotto

Ingredients:
- Cooked broad beans
- Diced carrots
- Finely chopped onions, shallots or leeks (can use all three)
- Olive oil
- Basmati rice
- Vegetable stock

Method:

1. Fry a combination of onions, shallots and / or leeks in a drop of olive oil until clear and / or tender.
2. Add the basmati rice and veg stock (1 cup of rice needs just over 1½ cups of stock).
3. Boil for 10 minutes, then allow to sit on an electric hob for a further 10 minutes. If gas, simmer for 20 minutes.
4. Add cooked broads and diced carrots for an attractive contrasting colour.
5. Toss and serve.

COURGETTES

COURGETTES

Courgettes with Onions

Ingredients:
- Oil
- 1 chopped medium white onion
- 3 chopped small courgettes (or 1 medium-sized) trimmed but not peeled
- Seasoning

Basically, the amount of courgette should be double that of the onion.

Method:
1. Fry onions in a drop of oil.
2. After only 1 or 2 minutes add chopped courgettes, then twist and shake of salt and pepper.
3. Cover pan and cook slowly to allow the moisture to come out of the courgettes.

Job done! This dish will always be sloppy but the amount of water in the dish may be reduced by frying hard at the end.

Lightly Spiced Courgettes

Ingredients:
- 900g medium or small courgettes, trimmed but not peeled
- 1 large white onion, peeled and grated
- 2 cloves garlic, peeled and chopped
- ½ teaspoon cayenne pepper
- 1 teaspoon paprika
- ½ teaspoon freshly ground black pepper
- 1 teaspoon cumin seeds (or ground cumin, 'jeera' powder)
- Salt to taste
- 6 tablespoons olive oil
- 6 tablespoons water

Garnish: chopped flat-leaved parsley or chopped green coriander leaves plus lemon juice.

Method:
1. Combine onion, garlic, cayenne, paprika, black pepper, cumin and salt in a bowl. Add olive oil and water then mix well.
2. Cut courgette into strips and place in a large frying pan.
3. Pour the onion, herb and spice mixture over them.
4. Cover pan and cook over a medium heat for about 20 minutes or until courgettes are tender.

LEEKS

Shallow Fried

Chop across the leek to create circles. Use all the blanched white stalk and a reasonable portion of the green uppers ('flag').

Pan fry with a knob of margarine for 5 to 10 minutes, then season with salt and pepper and eat whilst hot.

Braised

1. Remove the topper-most portion of flag and cut leeks lengthways.
2. Place in an ovenproof dish, cover with stock, pinch of salt and twist of pepper.
3. Braise in the oven at 200ºC (400ºF or Gas Mark 6) for 45 minutes.

With Mustard

Cook exactly as for Braised Leeks, except do not cover with stock. Instead, lavish the leeks with French mustard before placing in the oven with a lid on.

ONIONS

Crispy Fried, as a garnish

1. Slice any amount of white onions very finely. Place in a frying pan with oil, cook very slowly until translucent. Sprinkle salt and a little bit of sugar on them before frying hard and hot. Be alert as they will go from a perfect lovely brown to a nasty burned black very suddenly. You can't afford to look away even once!
2. Lift pan immediately from the heat, scoop onions onto a flat dinner plate.
3. The onions will be 'sticky' so use a fork in each hand to separate the strands with a deft touch. Spread them thinly so that none are on top of each other. When cooled they will be beautifully crisp and crunchy.

Perfect as a garnish for fried rice.

Onion Rings

Roll sliced onions in a mixture of flour, chilli powder, salt and pepper. Fry and eat hot!

As a Sauce

Fry chopped onions with chopped tomatoes at approximately equal quantities. Add salt, pepper, ginger powder and fry slowly as the tomatoes take a while to cook to a mush.

When oil becomes speckled with red spots (a sure sign that the tomatoes have cooked) add some water, bring to the boil and serve on mashed potato, spaghetti or boiled cauliflower.

ONIONS

Onion and Cauliflower Bhugia

Ingredients:
- Oil
- 1 onion sliced in rings
- 1 fresh or dried red chilli pod
- 1 cauliflower cut into florets
- Salt to taste
- 1 teaspoon cumin seeds
- 1 teaspoon sesame seeds
- 1 teaspoon fresh finely chopped ginger
- 1 chopped green chilli
- Fresh coriander leaves

Method:
1. Having fried the onion rings until pale, break red chilli pod into pieces over the onions and fry again.
2. Add cauliflower florets, ginger, green chilli and salt. Mix well, cover and cook on a low heat until the cauliflower is almost tender (stir occasionally to ensure even cooking).
3. Turn up the heat, add cumin and sesame seeds and stir briskly to get rid of any excess moisture.
4. Garnish with shredded coriander leaves (they must be well cut-up for their wonderful aroma to escape).

PARSNIP

Roasted

1. Scrub parsnips to remove all the earth. If large, then slice in half lengthways. Place on a tray and drizzle olive oil all over them, add seasoning and toss well to thoroughly coat. Do this bit by hand if needs-be.
2. Roast in the oven at 200°C (400°F or Gas Mark 6) for 45 minutes, or until golden-brown, in tandem with onions, butternut squash, potatoes - a feast!
3. Add whole garlic cloves in their skins about 20 minutes from the end of cooking time.

PARSNIP

Soup

Ingredients:
- 2 or 3 medium sized parsnips
- 1 or 2 onions
- 1 potato
- Margarine
- Flour
- Seasoning
- Mixed herbs
- Bouquet garni

Method:
1. Soak chopped onions in melted margarine for 10 minutes.
2. Boil the chopped parsnips, save the water.
3. Fry the onions, add parsnips and parsnip water, add diced potato.
4. Sprinkle light dustings of flour into the mix if it needs thickening until the consistency is as you want it.
5. Add seasoning, herbs and bouquet garni.
6. Boil for half-an-hour, blend and serve.

Taste can be varied by using different combinations of herbs or spices.

Soup with Apple

As above but use less onion.

When boiling add one peeled and chopped cooking ('culinary') or eating ('dessert') apple.

POTATO

Salt and Pepper
1. Peel 4 medium potatoes and chop quite small.
2. Heat oil in a frying pan, add potatoes and 1 teaspoon ground black pepper. Fry hard. Add a small amount of water, fry hard again until the water disappears.
3. Add salt to taste, fry hard. Add a small amount of water, fry hard again until all water disappears. Potatoes should be cooked and ready to eat by then.

Wedges
1. Cut 6 large spuds (not peeled) lengthways into 8 wedges each. Place in icy water for 30 minutes.
2. Remove spuds from the water, dry them and toss in olive oil. Arrange skin-side down on an oiled baking tray.
3. Mix together 1 tablespoon dried oregano, 1 teaspoon black pepper, salt to taste. Sprinkle this mixture over the oiled spuds and bake at 200°C (400°F or Gas Mark 6) for 50 minutes until golden-brown.

Curried
1. Peel and boil 4 large spuds, then cut into lengths (or quarters if using medium sized).
2. While they are cooking, peel and finely chop 2 onions and 2 garlic cloves. Fry them in oil adding 2 teaspoons turmeric (haldi), 2 teaspoons red chilli powder and salt to taste. Fry until brown then add a dollop of tomato ketchup.
3. Throw away half the water from the boiled spuds. Add the above mixture to spuds with their remaining water. Stir in well and bring to the boil before turning off (the more water you leave with the spuds the more gravy you will have; half is about enough).

SHALLOTS

Roasted with Couscous

Roast a combination of veggies including shallots, garlic, chick peas and peppers in the oven until tender. Put them on a flat tray and drizzle with olive oil, adding salt and pepper to taste.

Remove from the oven and add to prepared couscous. Stir together to mix well and serve hot or cold.

SQUASH AND PUMPKIN

Green Pumpkin Bhugia

Ingredients:
- Pumpkin (or squash), peeled and diced into small pieces
- 1 teaspoon cumin seeds
- Pinch dried methi (or ¼ teaspoon dried methi seeds)
- 1 teaspoon red chilli powder
- 1 teaspoon turmeric
- 1 teaspoon ground coriander (dhaniya)
- ½ teaspoon fennel seeds
- Salt
- ¼ teaspoon amchoor powder (dried ground mango)
- ⅛ teaspoon asafoetida powder (heeng)
- 1 tablespoon oil
- Sugar
- Fresh coriander

Method:
1. Heat oil, fry asafoetida first then immediately all the spices except amchoor powder.
2. Add the prepared pumpkin (or squash), cook slowly.
3. When pumpkin is cooked, after about 10 minutes, add amchoor powder plus a sprinkling of sugar.
4. Fry briefly and serve with finely chopped fresh coriander leaves.

SQUASH AND PUMPKIN

SQUASH AND PUMPKIN

Roasted Butternut

Method:
1. Slice butternut squash lengthways and then into quarters. Remove seeds and leave the skin on.
2. Place on a baking tray. Drizzle with olive oil, toss to coat. Add salt and pepper to taste.
3. Cook in oven at 200°C (400°F or Gas Mark 6) for 45 minutes.
4. Both the flesh and skin are edible and delicious.

Spicy Roasted

Use a winter squash (butternut or onion-type are especially good).

1. Make a mixture of 1 teaspoon each comprising ground coriander seeds and dried oregano, ½ teaspoon each of ground fennel seeds and black pepper, 1 teaspoon red chilli powder, pinch salt and 1 tablespoon of olive oil.
2. Cut squash lengthways and into quarters, remove seeds. Place on a baking tray, drizzle with olive oil and toss to coat.
3. Use fingers to apply the spice mixture to each piece of squash.
4. Roast at 200°C (400°F or gas Mark 6) for 45 minutes. Fresh squash means that the skin is easily edible so no scraping of flesh is required.

VARIOUS VEGGIES

VARIOUS VEGGIES

Summer Vegetable Pakoras

Ingredients:
- Gram flour, a sifted half-cup
- Turmeric, 1 teaspoon
- Chilli powder, 1 teaspoon
- Dhaniya powder (ground coriander seeds), 1½ teaspoon
- Salt to taste
- Heeng (ground asafoetida) – nicer if you have it but can do without. A pinch only to help with digestion as well as taste
- Dash or two of baking soda
- Plenty of oil
- Various vegetables including:
  - Very thinly sliced spuds
  - Florets of cauliflower
  - Florets of broccoli
  - Green beans
  - Single lettuce leaf
  - Single beet leaf or spinach
  - Chopped onion (if desired) mixed with chopped coriander and green chillies
  - Sliced aubergine (after salting and allowing moisture to come out)
  - Sliced courgettes

NOT peas, broad beans, corn off the cob as they cannot hold the batter.

Method:
Use enough gram flour for the amount of veg (start off with half a cup of flour) and blend together with all the spices, baking soda and water. Mix for a long time and beat it as if making a cake. This will allow the baking soda to work and make the mixture light and fluffy. It is easy to stop mixing too soon! The mixture needs to be thin enough to run off the vegetables yet thick enough for the batter to coat them before running off. The lightness and fluffiness helps to find this balance.

Heat 4 tablespoons of oil (to begin with, add more as and when required) in a frying pan. You can test the readiness of the oil by dropping a tiny drip of the gram flour mix into the oil. If it cooks (by going solid) right away then the oil is hot enough and ready.

Use various combinations of veg individually. Drag them through the batter and flop into the frying pan. Cook on medium to hot, ensuring that the oil cooks the veg through but does not burn gram flour coating before doing so. For leaves, cooking is virtually instantaneous. For florets, it is a bit longer.

GLOSSARY OF TERMS

ANNUAL (WEED): plant that completes its life cycle in one season.

ARABLE (FARMLAND): land used to grow crops.

BLANCH: in cooking, to plunge vegetables into boiling water to tenderise them and preserve their natural colour; in gardening, to exclude light to cause whiteness of produce.

BLIGHT: fungal disease affecting especially potatoes and tomatoes.

BLOSSOM-END ROT: sunken, brown flower-end of curcubits and tomatoes.

BRASSICA: any member of the cabbage tribe.

BROADCAST-SOW: scatter seeds by hand over an area as opposed to sowing in rows.

BUSH (APPLE): has an open centre branching from a trunk at about 90 cm.

CATKIN (HAZEL): the male flowers that look like dangling lambs' tails.

CHIT (POTATOES): to set the individual spuds out so that shoots develop.

CHOKE (ARTICHOKE): the portion inside the bud which would develop into the petals.

CLAMP: method of storing veggies outdoors by covering with a mound of soil and straw to over-winter, or more simply with just soil.

CLOCHE: a clear covering for early and late veg protection which is portable.

COMPOST: an organic material made up principally of decomposed vegetable matter.

CROWN (ARTICHOKE, ASPARAGUS): base of the plant at ground level or just below.

CURCUBITS: cucumbers, squashes, marrows and courgettes.

DIRECT-SOWING: the act of sowing seeds straight into the ground as opposed to rearing seedlings in pots.

EARTH-UP: to draw soil up around the base of a plant, integral to potato cultivation but also applicable to leeks, celery, carrots and others.

EPHEMERAL (WEEDS): plants that produce numerous generations in a season.

FAN-TRAINED (MORELLO CHERRY OR OTHER FRUIT): to persuade a woody plant to grow flat against a fence or wall with branches spread as a fan.

FIRST-EARLY (POTATO): quick maturing variety of spud which is ready to dig in June.

FIRST THINNING: the initial act of removing excess seedlings and weaklings following sowing.

FLAG (LEEK): the leaves at the top of the plant.

FLORET: small flower head (of broccoli or cauliflower).

FORK-IN: using a garden fork to disturb and turn the soil surface.

FRIABLE SOIL: soil that is easily broken down into crumbs.

GARDENER'S SHUFFLE: small sideways steps taken forwards and backwards to firm a bed, principally before planting onion sets or brassicas.

GERMINATION: this is what happens when a seed first starts to develop into a plant.

GRAFT: the act of joining two separate parts of different plants together.

GREEN MANURE: a quick-growing cover crop grown to replenish nutrients and body in a soil, protect it, or both.

GREY MOULD (BOTRYTIS): grey or off-white fungal fuzz on crops, especially prone in a poorly ventilated greenhouse.

GROWBAG: plastic bag containing compost specially designed for the direct cultivation of a range of vegetables.

HALF-STANDARD (APPLE): one that has 1–1.5 metres of clear stem before branching occurs.

HARDEN OFF: the act of putting young crops from the greenhouse or windowsill outside during late-spring daytimes but bringing them under cover at night to acclimatise them.

HAULM (POTATO): the stems and leaves above ground (also used to describe similar in tomatoes).

HEEL-IN: to dig a rough hole or trench for short-term storage of bare-rooted trees, brassicas and leeks.

HONEYDEW: plant sap excreted by an aphid.

IN-THE-GREEN: term used to describe bulbous plants such as snowdrops when leaves are fully formed.

LEAFMOULD: decomposed leaves used as a soil conditioner.

LEGUME: members of the pea and bean family with nitrogen-rich nodules on their roots.

LIQUID FERTILISER: concentrated liquid goodness which can be added to water for feeding crops, commonly made from nettles and comfrey.

MAINCROP: varieties of vegetables which produce the bulk of the crop in the main growing season.

MAINCROP (POTATO): spuds that mature over the course of the summer and are ready for digging from August onwards (blight permitting).

MULCH: protective layer of material placed on top of the soil and / or around plants to suppress weeds and conserve moisture.

MULTI-PURPOSE COMPOST: compost purchased in bags from the garden centre which suits any job from sowing seeds to raising crops in containers.

NOCTURNAL: active at night-time.

NURSERY BED: special area where crops are nurtured from the seedling stage until big enough to withstand life in the main bed.

PERENNIAL (WEED): one that comes back year after year from reserves stored in a fleshy or extensive root system.

PLANT-UP: to plant individual specimens into their final resting places, either on the plot or in grow-bags.

POT-ON / UP: to transfer seedlings into a bigger pot.

POTTING COMPOST: same as multi-purpose compost.

PRICKING-OUT: to carefully remove seedlings from a seed tray into individual pots.

ROOT-BALL: in container-grown plants, the knot of roots and growing medium in the pot or container.

ROOT NODULES: found on members of the pea and bean family, these distortions are home for nitrogen-fixing bacteria.

ROOTSTOCK: the part of a grafted plant (usually a fruit tree) which provides the roots.

ROSE (WATERING CAN): the fitting on the spout which filters water into a fine spray.

SALTING: the process of sprinkling salt onto veg to extract the moisture.

SCORCHING (OF LEAVES): happens when strong sunlight is magnified by water droplets on the leaf and it burns.

SECOND-EARLY (POTATO): early maturing variety ready to dig in July.

SEEDBED: ground prepared to a fine tilth for direct-sowing of seeds.

SEED-LEAVES: the initial pair of leaves which appear after germination.

SEEDLING: the name given to a plant in the early stages of growth.

SEED POTATO: usually certified disease-free, these individuals are the source of the potato crop and normally available in the shops from January (you can save your own, but there is a high disease risk).

SPEAR (ASPARAGUS): the much-prized and utterly delicious phallic shoot which is cut and eaten through late-April to early-June.

SPIT: in gardening terms, this is the length of a garden spade-head.

STANDARD (APPLE): a tree with about 2 metres of bare stem before branching.

STANDING CROPS: any crops which are ready to eat and are stored where they grew in the ground until harvest-time.

STATION-SOW: the act of sowing a few seeds together at regular intervals along a row as opposed to sowing thinly in a line.

STEP-OVER (APPLE): a variety grown on dwarfing rootstock as a single spread of two opposite branches trained horizontally about 30 cm above the ground.

SUCCESSION-SOWING: sowing varieties of veg at intervals, say fortnightly, to ensure a long cropping period.

SUMMER-PRUNE (APPLES AND PEARS): cutting out woody stems to inhibit growth.

TASSEL (SWEETCORN): the female flower which forms as swollen tufts along the stalk.

TIE-IN: in fruit trees and tomatoes, the act of tying branches and stems to supports.

TILTH: of soil, the fine crumbly surface created by cultivation.

TOP-DRESS: to apply a material to the soil surface to replenish body or nutrients.

TOP-FRUIT: apples and pears.

TRANSLUCENT: almost see-through.

TUBER: a fleshy stem or root in which a plant stores reserves of food, usually underground.

UMBEL: a cluster of tiny flowers arising from the same point on stems the same length.

WIND-ROCK: damage caused by the wind, especially low down at the crown.

WINTER-PRUNE (APPLES AND PEARS): cutting out dead, diseased and overcrowded branches to maintain an open centre to the tree and encourage growth.

INDEX